At Forthview Primary School, we believe education should touch the whole child/person. This includes the physical, emotional, spiritual, social and cognitive aspects of the child's life. We teach children quietness as a skill to reflect and recharge their inner lives. Lorraine Murray of Feel Good Therapies helped us on this journey.

- Lorraine taught groups of children to be still, relax and meditate. She worked skilfully with a wide spectrum of children including those with ADHD – not easy in a quiet room!
- Lorraine ran well-received, regular sessions in relaxation and Reiki to improve staff well-being.
- We wanted to increase the capacity of school staff to work with children in this way and so Lorraine successfully taught a group of staff how to teach children relaxation and meditation. This staff group then took over from Lorraine in teaching children during our special 'multiple intelligence Golden Time' at Forthview.
- Feel Good Therapies' input enhanced the life of our school and I highly recommend them.

Sheila Laing, former Head Teacher,
Forthview Primary School, Edinburgh

Calm Kids

Help Children Relax
with Mindful Activities

LORRAINE E. MURRAY

Floris Books

An important note:
Lorraine E. Murray is not a medical doctor. The ideas in this book are based on her experience of working with children. They may complement, but should never replace, the advice and treatment of a medical specialist. If you are concerned about your child's health, please consult a medical doctor.

First published in 2012 by Floris Books
© 2012 Lorraine Murray
Illustrations © BCG Web Design Ltd.
& Feel Good Therapies Ltd.

Lorraine Murray has asserted her right under the
Copyright, Designs and Patent Act 1988
to be identified as the author of this work

British Library CIP Data available
ISBN 978-086315-862-9

Printed in Great Britain
by CPI Group (UK) Ltd, Croydon

FSC
www.fsc.org
MIX
Paper from
responsible sources
FSC® C013604

Contents

For all the children around the world – may you be guided to realise the peace you carry in your hearts.

If your plan is for one year, plant rice. If your plan is for ten years, plant trees. If your plan is for one hundred years, educate children.

Confucius

Introduction

My daughter did her first meditation today. She loved it and couldn't believe what she saw. She only did it for five minutes but found it amazing. Thanks for all your help.

Parent

Hello and welcome to this book, which I hope will bring some peace and harmony not only into the lives of your children, but into your life too.

I appreciate that as a parent or anyone who works with children, your time is precious and there is usually not enough of it! That's why you have my sincerest thanks for buying this book. It will help you share time with your children in a positive and enlightening way.

First of all let me be clear, I am not yet a parent. However I am an auntie, a godmother and a friend of many people with children of all ages, and these roles allow me to observe how people interact with their children from a holistic perspective. I do not judge anyone but simply 'see' this through my teaching experience, having worked with meditation and healing for many years.

I realised very early on that children are unique. Each child is a walking, talking, breathing, sleeping collection of energy that is as beautiful as it is individual. Whilst we may think that as parents and teachers we are here to guide children and that it's pretty much a one-way street for most of their younger lives, the truth is that it's a two-way street. They learn and you learn. Sometimes the lessons are easy and beautiful, and sometimes the lessons are hard and challenging. But the relationship with your children is a precious jewel that needs attention, care and a level of understanding from the heart as well as the head. That's why I felt compelled to write this book.

The idea of teaching children how to meditate came early on, just before I set up my business teaching meditation to adults, running courses in healing and massage whilst practising as an aromatherapist. After I returned from a holiday in Canada, I noticed that the media seemed to talk about nothing else but how stressed children were, whether it was from bullying, school or just life in general. I thought at the time, 'Wouldn't it be great if we could teach children simple methods of dealing with stress like meditation?' My thinking was that it would help them through these challenges, rather than waiting until they grew into adulthood and then having to unpick all the 'damage' from the past before they could live peaceful lives.

I set about exploring these ideas. I had been teaching adults but knew nothing about working with children. I was fortunate to meet an inspirational, local head teacher who liked the idea of teaching children these methods and allowed me to run 'relaxation and meditation' sessions in their quiet room. To help you understand, this school is in one of the most socially challenged and difficult areas of Edinburgh. These children were the starting point and I am eternally grateful to them for what they taught me.

My work took me into other schools and I was also asked to run sessions for staff, teaching them how to run meditation sessions with children. I even asked friends if I could borrow their children so I could test ideas with them to see how they responded to certain techniques. All the while these experiences helped me to build up my knowledge of the differences and similarities between teaching children and adults meditation.

I developed a meditation CD based on my findings, and have received wonderful feedback about it so I felt encouraged to continue. I then started to receive phone calls from people asking me how to teach these meditation methods to children. This got me thinking and I decided to write this book so I could consolidate all I have learned and present it to you in a practical way for you to use and enjoy.

In addition to all this, I continued to teach meditation (and other complementary therapies) to adults in private classes. It was during this time that I noticed how adults progress in their meditation practice. They sometimes start off being very 'ungrounded', which means they can't keep their feet flat on the ground or they fidget (see section on the 'Importance of Grounding', p.38). However by week three or four of our course, they became much more settled and would often comment on how this had a positive impact on their lives: they were more able to focus and complete tasks; they had more energy and slept better etc. I can't recall exactly why this led me to make a connection between ADHD (Attention Deficit Hyperactivity Disorder), but it did. In my experience, many of the 'symptoms' of being ungrounded are very similar to those displayed by children who have ADHD. I decided to explore this a little further with the help of willing clients who had children with ADHD.

This also led me on to the issue of the autistic spectrum. What a huge area of opinion this is! I can assure you I have not covered all aspects. However I came across many parents whose children were struggling with the condition, so I decided to explore and research this area too. I recalled listening to a lecture given by Raun Kaufman, son of the founders of the Son-Rise Program, which offers a treatment and educational model for anyone working with (or who have) children with autism. Raun was diagnosed as autistic but the programme his parents founded in 1974 helped him recover from his autism. He gave an excellent lecture and many of the things he spoke about struck a chord with me from a meditation perspective. This encouraged me to believe that meditation and mindful activities had some part to play in helping both children on the autistic spectrum and their families. In this book I share some of these ideas, some of which I have tested with children who have Asperger syndrome.

The research in this book is not conclusive and it is not meant to be. I have realised that there is no 'one size fits all' solution. Just as I said that all children are unique, autistic children are even more so! But they have a beautiful gift to share. I hope that meditation can be one of the keys to help you unlock this gift and show their true potential, whilst revealing your potential too.

Finally, I decided to include some information for people with babies and toddlers. At the beginning of my work with children, I believed that children need to cognitively understand before you can teach them how to meditate, however I've since changed my mind. To be honest, meditation with babies is more for mums and dads with newborns. It's a very stressful time for everyone involved and the methods are to help new parents feel calm. Their calmness then influences the baby and, if nothing else, gives parents something new to try when all else fails.

Mindful activities with toddlers are more playful and active than meditating with older children. They are calming, which is helpful as part of the bedtime routine. For information, I would class toddlers as from around two to three years old, but remember that every child's development is different so pick any methods that suit your child.

It's important to me that this book is practical and accessible to people with all levels of ability. Even if you are completely new to meditation, you will find simple methods that do not require any previous experience. However if you are familiar with meditation, you will enjoy the book too.

One of my inspirational teachers, Kim McManus, helped me realise that meditation is simply a very practical tool for life that empowers you with a positive awareness of yourself, the world and your place in it.

If there is one key message I can give to you it is that meditation is a personal journey. No matter what age, background or experience, we should allow each other (and especially our children) to discover this. Please do not force any activity on them because you think it's a great idea. Although it helps to have some kind of structure and discipline, which this book provides, none of us likes to be dragged into doing something we don't want to do. Encourage your children to choose from the different techniques and help them to decide which methods they can learn to feel calmer, happier and more peaceful. I have tried to provide a variety of ideas to get you started so that there's plenty to choose from, but you can adapt these to suit your needs.

Finally, as all of us travel on this road of learning, remember that the end destination is not the goal. The 'goal' of meditation is being aware of each step, learning to appreciate it for what it is: an opportunity to grow. I am still learning. I hope you are too.

1. What Is Meditation?

I have my two-year-old take deep breaths when he's finding it hard to cope with emotions or is simply overexcited. I add a visual clue to help him determine that he's breathing in or out deeply by having him blow at my hair on the out-breath and making it move. I, in turn, do the same to him and this seems to help him slow down, smile and recognise the required action by its simple reaction.

Parent

The word 'meditation' has many different interpretations. For some people it has become synonymous with the idea of 'relaxation' or 'stress management'. When I was first introduced to meditation, I had no idea what to expect and perhaps you feel that way too. Or perhaps you have tried something like meditation in your yoga classes.

For me, meditation is very simple – it's about being in the moment. In that moment I have a level of awareness that allows me just to be in the experience of life and let go of the inner tension that builds up as a result of my thoughts or feelings. For me, meditation is about focus in the 'here and now', where I can simply enjoy physical sensations or my breath, or I can be guided on a peaceful journey using visual imagery or my other inner senses.

Adults tend to spend a lot of time analysing and judging life (and themselves) rather than just being in the moment. This is why teaching children meditation can be easier than teaching adults. The young mind is much more open. With children there are usually no logical barriers that interrupt meditation. However, the following explanation can help your logical mind to adjust to this non-logical experience we call 'meditation'.

A factual explanation of meditation

It is a fact that we (children and adults) experience different states of consciousness during our daily lives – sleep, full alertness and being half asleep or daydreaming.

However, did you know that the brain's frequency of electrical energy changes depending on our state of awareness? This frequency has been measured by scientists using an EEG (electroencephalograph), which measures the various levels of electrical activity in the brain during different states of consciousness. The measurement of this activity is in hertz (waves per second).

Full-alert mode

When children are completely awake their brain frequency is usually between 15–30 hertz (Hz). This is called the *Beta state* and it's where they do most of their daily activity – playing, schoolwork, talking and so on. This is the state of awareness we are all in when we're conscious of the outside world, e.g. when reading this book.

Daydreamer

Then we have the *Alpha state* which, from a meditation perspective, is very useful to nurture in children. With children's brains operating at 9–14 Hz during the Alpha state of consciousness, they can notice their surroundings without 'thinking and analysing', just simply enjoying and being in the experience. I compare it to the state we feel when we're in bed just before we go to sleep, as we notice how warm, comfortable and relaxing the bed is and how safe and good it feels to be there. Or perhaps when we're enjoying a beautiful scene in nature – a sunset or a peaceful forest – where we're absorbed by the beauty of our surroundings and stop thinking our usual busy thoughts.

The Alpha state is the level of awareness we encourage children to experience during meditation, and is the state adult beginners in meditation can reach with practice.

A waking dream

After the Alpha state our consciousness moves into a deeper state of awareness called the *Theta state,* which has a frequency of 4–8 Hz. Here there is no 'thought'. All of us experience this to some degree. This is the deeper consciousness state associated with deep sleep and dreaming. With practice, this state of consciousness can be reached, however it is more suited to adults, whose brains are fully developed neurologically. Some experienced meditation practitioners enter this state with a question to access solutions and answers. It takes practice to enter this state in meditation, but it's something that we all experience fleetingly as we go in and out of our deeper sleep state.

In this Theta state we can still be awakened or 'brought back' by a noise or sound in our environment. The Theta state is perhaps the state that many parents with newborns find themselves in during those first six months when the baby's cries awaken them. It's also referred to as the dream state, where you actively dream. I think of Theta as being the precursor to the final sleep state of Delta.

Deep sleep

The *Delta state* is the deep sleep state. The frequency of our brain activity here is a gentle 1–3 Hz. During this time our body cells go into regeneration mode, where our body physically 'heals' and comes back into balance. This is where we have a dreamless sleep.

Spirituality and inner balance

I have noticed an increased level of interest in meditation in recent years, whether it's based on a spiritual quest or a de-stressing technique. However meditation is not a new 'fad' but a practice that reaches back thousands of years in some cultures, although by comparison it is relatively new to us in the West. Many meditation practices are still associated with religious or spiritual beliefs, but in the West we are waking up to the health benefits of practising mindfulness meditation techniques.

You probably bought this book to help your children to be calm. Although this is one reason, just consider that helping your children to meditate will also give you the space for some calmness too and the opportunity to bond with your children in a way where you both connect 'in the moment'.

In my experience, regardless of what logical reason you can apply to an interest in meditation, there is a deeper spiritual part within each of us that drives us towards balance and peace and which meditation helps us to discover. If you know how to meditate but are not practising it regularly then this book will help you and your children to make that time.

This 'inner drive' in our children (and us) towards balance and peace is very similar to how their physical bodies heal. If children cut their fingers, they don't tell their bodies to clot the blood, seal the wound and send cells to fight infection. Their bodies know what they need to do to come back into balance and they do this as well as they can. When children meditate, they help themselves to come back into balance mentally, emotionally and spiritually as naturally as the healing of a cut finger.

2. Understanding Stress

For every minute you are angry you lose sixty seconds of happiness.

Ralph Waldo Emerson

What is stress?

The word 'stress' is overused and many people don't realise how important it is for their well-being and survival. Quite simply, we can't live without stress! A short burst of stress is known as the 'stress response' and more commonly as the 'flight or fight' syndrome. It is as natural to have this response as breathing. If we didn't have this response, our bodies wouldn't be able to react to danger, by either running away or fighting the attacker – both of which require our muscles to tense, our heart to beat faster and our circulation to be redirected to the necessary parts of our bodies.

When reacting to stress, other automatic bodily processes go on 'behind the scenes': our adrenal glands release adrenaline and other hormones and chemicals, such as cortisol, to help us respond to the stressor; our blood vessels narrow and we sweat to regulate body temperature. Even our nails and hair stop growing, as this isn't an important function when faced with danger.

This reaction is called 'acute stress' and after the stressor has passed, the body starts to go back into normal mode. This response has helped the human race to survive, so in these circumstances, stress is good.

However, there are a couple of other aspects to stress. First of all, if the threat doesn't disappear, then the body sustains the stress response, thereby never returning to normal. Put simply, if our muscles are tense and never get to relax, then the circulation around the muscles can't remove toxins and nourish the cells with oxygen as effectively – and we might experience a build up of tension and eventually chronic pain. Secondly, the threat may not be real. In other words we perceive that a person or a situation is threatening, but this may not be correct. If we are facing a sabre-tooth tiger, then yes the danger is real. Or if we have to manage a bullying colleague at work or a difficult marriage then the threat can be real. However we may have started a new job or just become a new parent, which are classic opportunities to experience the stress response as we try to cope with this new challenge. The 'threat' in these circumstances comes from our own perception and the pressure we place upon ourselves.

I have worked with lots of parents and find that the pressure on them to be 'good parents' doesn't always come from outside but from their own internal dialogue and how they 'see' themselves through the eyes of others. They are not in fact seeing themselves in a true sense: as a new parent who will make mistakes and learn, and so on. Even for parents who have several children, each child is unique, so the parenting experience is an ongoing learning curve.

I have put together this simple list of the stress responses and the effects of short- and long-term stress.

Summary of stress responses

Please note that this is a simplified example and not a medical diagnosis.

Acute stress response	Chronic stress response	Response after taking steps to reduce stress
Increase in muscle tension (limbs, solar plexus)	Unable to relax, muscle pain	Muscles start to relax and tension released
Blood supply redirected away from digestive system	Digestive problems – constipation, diarrhoea	Blood supply improves – often hear 'gurgling tummies' during a meditation session
Blood supply redirected away from skin	Pale skin, skin problems	Skin problems reduce

Increase in the release of glucose (energy) into our blood stream	Over-stimulation of glucose in body – problems sleeping, may lead to diabetes or energy fluctuations (e.g. ME)	Energy levels more balanced, sleep improves
Heart beats faster	Heart overworked, heart conditions	Heart returns to normal rhythm
Increase in blood pressure as blood vessels constrict to help blood move around the body	Potential for high blood pressure	Blood pressure can start to stabilise
Body begins to sweat	Regular fluctuations in body temperature	Body temperature returns to normal
Release of cortisol into the blood stream	Excess amounts of cortisol – crying, very emotional	Feel more emotionally balanced
Breathing gets faster to take in more oxygen	Breathing problems, anxiety	Breath becomes calmer and more relaxed

Acknowledging our own stress levels

The good news is that even if we have reached a state of chronic stress, we can start to reverse the symptoms by practising relaxation, meditation and mindful activities. Whilst you may have bought this book on the basis of supporting your children, this is a great opportunity for you to acknowledge your own stress levels. When I was writing this book, I realised there was a 'chicken and egg' scenario at play. Whilst helping your children to meditate, you will be able to sense your own stress, start to relax and let go. And the more you learn how to relax and stay calm, the more this positively influences your children. Parents have assured me that their children seem to reflect back their parents' state of mind and energy, particularly when they are stressed.

Perhaps you don't realise that you're stressed. Often it's hard to admit it. Society seems to encourage us to just soldier on regardless of whether we're experiencing changes, such us moving home, change of jobs, economic problems, terrorist attacks, house renovations, dealing with the grief of death or a long-term illness. Lots of people live life with minds full of worrying thoughts or a constant feeling of anxiety. In these circumstances, we can gradually slip into a long-term stress state, and it's not until the symptoms become severe that we pay any attention to our health. I'm not suggesting that we can avoid these changes (perceived threats), as this is life! However by practising meditation you can find ways to change how you view the world. I speak from personal experience when I say that meditation is an excellent tool to help you see the world differently and more positively – from a wider perspective – and therefore reduce the effects of long-term stress.

Stress in children

I like it when my teacher is nice to me, it makes my brain happy.

Sienna, age 5

Sometimes adults don't realise that children experience stress too. We may have rosy coloured memories of childhood where life seemed simpler. In today's world our children are bombarded with pressurised marketing campaigns that encourage them to grow up quickly or desire products they don't always need, and over-exposure to computer games that may potentially distort their awareness of reality.

There are the pressures of school, exams and peer pressure. Plus, children feel and sense their parents' stress (or that of any adults around them) and learn from adults how to cope (or not cope) with stress. It may seem that your children are unaware of your stress or may not understand the words you use when you complain to friends about money worries and so on, but they understand your tone of voice and they sense the pressures that adults feel. They sense your stress in addition to experiencing challenges in their own lives.

I have suggested some perceived threats that children might feel or experience.

Perceived threats experienced by children and teenagers

- Listening to parents argue
- Falling out with friends
- Being bullied
- Unable to do homework
- Hearing about money issues from adults
- Listening to the news

- Not having the most up-to-date toy, clothes or gadget
- Not being able to sleep
- Being scared of the dark
- Sibling rivalry
- Being abandoned – fear of something happening to parents
- Parents being intoxicated on drugs or alcohol
- No one to play with

Compared to adults, children don't know how to recognise stress or how to cope with and process it. They often don't have the vocabulary or opportunity to express these feelings. I believe that if we don't start supporting our children with tools for life that help them to identify, express and process these thoughts, then the next generation will contain many more angry and frustrated people. Meditation and mindfulness help children to become aware of their feelings and process them safely, releasing emotions so that they don't build up inside and spiral into a lifelong 'tantrum'.

I do a guided meditation with my daughter to help her go to sleep (I know that mediation isn't 'meant' to induce sleep but it helps her settle down when she's having trouble going off to the land of nod). I don't know if it would work for others, but it definitely works for my daughter!

Parent

3. The Benefits of Meditation for Children

My eleven-year-old son has just started meditation after having a hard time at school. He's finding it all much easier to cope with now. I just wish every child could do this!

Parent

There are some clear reasons why helping children learn meditation can benefit them in the short and long term. Earlier I discussed the different levels of awareness in our consciousness – Alpha and Theta – which are a key aspect of meditation (see p.14). Both levels of awareness have benefits, however I suggest that you focus on exploring the Alpha state when working with children. The Alpha level of meditation is an accessible way for all of us, including our children, to meditate as part of our normal routine.

Practising the Alpha state through meditation encourages children to use their imagination or to explore the world through their senses in a way which is 'relaxed but alert'. It helps them to nurture their ability to focus and concentrate rather then being easily distracted by their thoughts or environment. It helps them to control their 'butterfly mind', and it can help children to unwind before going to bed, helping them to sleep. If you teach your children this level of awareness, they will have an empowering skill that will help them to manage stress and life.

Improving sleep

This must be a positive benefit not only for your child but for you! Meditation and mindfulness help to retrain the mind and body back into an Alpha state, which encourages longer and improved sleep. In our courses people often report that they are sleeping more soundly or longer as a result of practising meditation.

For younger children (age 6 or younger), simple relaxation techniques before going to bed can become part of their established bedtime routines, helping them to move into their deeper sleep state (see pp.44, 102). I often recommend that if you're using meditation methods to help directly improve sleep, you should do this together when they're lying down in bed. It's similar to telling your children a bedtime story, helping to use their imagination and the part of the brain that enables them to switch off and into the Alpha state.

Managing thoughts and feelings

Learning meditation helps children cope with challenges – encouraging their minds to develop positive filters of their experiences and use this positive view to perceive the world. Meditation teaches children how to stay grounded, let go of negative thoughts, process negative feelings and not become overwhelmed by normal aspects of life, like sitting exams or studying.

When I worked at the Maggie's Cancer Caring Centres in Edinburgh, helping to teach meditation and stress management, I heard the following analogy, which I thought was a good example of how meditation supports the mind and emotions:

> Think about a puppy on an autumn day... it sees all the leaves blowing around and all it wants to do is chase them. The owner wants to train the puppy so that it will watch the leaves but refrain from chasing them. With practice and training, the owner teaches the puppy to observe the leaves but leave them alone.

This analogy represents learning meditation. Consider that your child's mind is the puppy, the leaves are thoughts and feelings and the puppy owner is the child. Meditation teaches children how to observe their thoughts and feelings but not become lost or overwhelmed in them.

Practising meditation regularly helps children to manage their thoughts and feelings, and offers them the potential to gain a more positive attitude towards life. It teaches them how to step back and develop a different perspective of their experiences – one not so consumed by their thoughts and emotions. This is a very empowering step, when someone is able to perceive life more objectively in this way. With practice, your children can gradually allow this level of awareness and strength of mind to positively influence how they feel *at any moment and in any situation*. They can learn how to stay calm, focused, grounded and objective, to avoid repeating negative experiences. Or if they do have a wobble and a strong reaction to a challenge, meditation can help them to reflect on the experience and learn from it, so that they can choose an appropriate response to future situations. I have experienced this; it's not just a theory. In the past I've faced challenging situations or people that pressed my buttons and left me feeling angry, hurt or anxious. Through meditation, I've learned to remain calm, grounded and strong in similar situations – or to reflect on the lesson of the experience and see how I can change my responses in the future.

Building self-esteem

Another of the issues our children face is a lack of self-esteem. Self-esteem comes from children knowing who they are and their purpose and place in this world. It builds through children's experiences (both positive and negative) so that they can learn and grow. It comes from learning that what you choose to say, do or be has an outcome and connects you to the rest of the world. It comes from knowing that whatever happens on the outside, children can learn to choose their response on the inside. When children practise meditation they become aware of those choices and responses. That awareness feeds their foundation of self-esteem and spiritual power, helping them to understand their place in this world and who they truly are. What greater gift can we give children than this strong foundation of self-esteem that will support them throughout life?

Learning to relax

An important first step in learning meditation is simply learning to relax. Learning to relax helps your child (and you) to take baby steps towards meditation. It helps the body, mind and emotions to unwind and prepare your child for mindful activities. I find it easier to teach relaxation to children than adults because the logical adult mind gets in the way. You may find that your child is tightly wound up or very energetic, so even if you don't manage to get your child to go any further, it's worth practising relaxation exercises again and again, until you both feel ready to try meditation. Don't dismiss this important first step. The more you both learn to relax and let go, the more easily your child will step into meditation.

Relaxation is an excellent precursor to sleep, and you may find that you use relaxation methods with your children whilst they are lying down in bed. However, in general when I talk about relaxation, I don't mean lying down exhausted on the floor and falling asleep. I mean the ability to relax and let go whilst awake; for your child to be relaxed and alert when eating dinner, speaking to you, drawing or painting, playing in the garden, or helping you to make dinner.

Being relaxed and alert is a key step for you too as you are the one teaching your children to meditate. If you are uptight or stressed, then your children will not relax. So as you take them through the relaxation, listen to the words and follow them too. You can practise being relaxed but alert whilst sitting at your computer, sitting in traffic, waiting to cross the road, hanging out the washing or making dinner. I call this process of learning to relax whilst being alert, 'becoming self-aware' (see p.72).

You may think that your children will find it impossible to relax or perhaps you're thinking this will be easy! Each child is different so some may relax more easily than others. Remember that they're living, breathing human beings, whose emotions, thoughts and physical energy vary from day to day, and moment to moment. The same applies to you. Some days it will be easy to relax and other times it will feel harder. Just trying (regardless of how you or your child feel) is important and do not judge the outcome. It's important to let go of any judgements and negative thoughts, as they may prevent you from progressing. Relaxation and meditation are all about regular, gentle practice. Think of 'learning to relax' like the warm-up before sport, preparing you for the next step.

Having more balanced energy

The process of becoming relaxed helps our bodies to unwind and release some of the stress held within. You may not realise that our physical bodies, emotions and thoughts are all connected, so 'simply relaxing' is more than that – it's an opportunity for our physical bodies to let go, allowing our emotions and thoughts to come into balance. For example, as children relax their bodies, the muscles that were holding tension start to let go, and blood circulation improves, allowing the blood to do its job of taking oxygen to the cells and removing toxins. The more oxygen their cells receive the more energy they have, so they will feel more refreshed, balanced and alert. Children might become aware of what they're feeling and thinking at this moment, but as each feeling or thought comes up they learn to 'let it go'. They are actively bringing their energy into balance.

As children relax, their circulation also starts to flow more effectively into areas like the digestive system. When I teach meditation classes, I often hear a few grumbling tummies when we start to relax and (if it's not hunger related) it's usually a sign that students' bodies are relaxing as they come back into balance and let go of the day's tension that they hold around the digestive area.

Improved focus and concentration

After practising the enjoyable step of relaxation, children can benefit from learning how to focus and concentrate. The techniques explained in this book will help children to keep their minds focused on an object. The object can be their breath, a physical object (like a stone), a word, a guided imaginary journey or using one of their five senses. Practising focus helps children to stop their minds from darting around and being easily distracted, allowing them to complete tasks more easily. As children become aware of their thoughts through meditation, they can start to take gentle steps to refocus their minds. People in my meditation classes often comment on feeling more 'grounded' or 'focused' when they practise meditation after only three or four sessions.

Gently encouraging the mind to become stronger and more focused is important for studying. Through meditation you will also help children to tap into their own creativity and imagination, which in turn will help them to discover solutions to problems and challenges they face in life.

Peaceful mind, peaceful body, peaceful life

Thoughts can affect our physiological well-being, so if our children are worried about something it can affect their bodies too – tummy upsets being a classic example. To change the way we think (e.g. to stop worrying) we first have to become aware of the problem: we become aware *then* we choose different thoughts. Only through awareness can we choose to change.

Remember that children are influenced by their experiences and the world around them. So if they think negatively 'the world is a threatening/difficult place' (glass is half empty) or positively 'the world is a loving place/life is good' (glass is half full), these thoughts will influence how they feel and behave in the world. Let me give you an example of how our physical bodies and thoughts are connected, and how meditation helps to process emotions and change your child's way of thinking:

> You sit down to meditate with your children and they notice that their shoulders are sore. You try the relaxation methods but you find that they become more aware of the tension and pain in their shoulders. As you encourage them to breathe into the area of their body you ask them to notice how they feel. They notice how irritated they feel. You ask them to breathe into those feelings and notice any thoughts that spring to mind of something someone has said or done to upset them. They continue to breathe into this area of their body and the associated feelings, and as they notice the negative thoughts you ask them to let them go with each out-breath. Perhaps you then ask them to choose a more positive thought with the in-breath and continue to let go of negative thoughts with the out-breath. As they start to do this, the tension in their shoulders starts to ease.

By showing children this approach you are giving them the ability to positively affect their thoughts and feelings, and in turn their quality of life and life choices. This creates a positive behaviour cycle, informing all future decisions and responses. This is powerful stuff!

Perhaps you're thinking that you'd prefer your children not to notice how busy or negative their minds are and simply to shut out all these thoughts and have some peace and quiet! Suppressing worries can work in the short term, but meditation gives children long-term support as they learn to change through awareness, using mindful activities for a sense of inner peace.

'I think, therefore I am.'

René Descartes

4. Creating a Relaxing Environment

I have done guided meditation with my seven-year-old – I love helping children to grow up free from the 'stuff' that would stop them manifesting anything they want when they grow up, most importantly self-esteem, happiness, love.

Parent

It helps to create an environment that signals to your children, using all five senses, that this is a time for relaxation and meditation, so they learn to switch into this more relaxed state.

These tips on creating the optimum setting will help to support children in relaxation, and then allow you to proceed towards meditation sessions of 5–20 minutes. These tips don't apply to really short exercises, such as focusing on the breath for a minute, or using day-to-day activities like brushing hair or teeth, which are all about strengthening the focus in a normal day-to-day routine.

The following sections contain suggestions for your information and consideration. However, if trying to create the right environment feels overwhelming, don't let it deter you from trying. Simply pick and choose what you can accommodate and start practising. There are no mistakes in meditation – only experiences.

Do not disturb

It's important that phones are switched off. Do not even have your phone on silent or vibrate as some music systems will pick up a message through the speakers, which will start to buzz – it's really distracting! If possible, try to meditate in a room that doesn't have a phone. If other people are in the house, ask them to be quiet. Ask them to turn the TV down, even hang a 'Shhh... we are meditating' sign on the door! You could ask your child to help design and draw a sign.

Using sight

For meditation and relaxation it's best to use low lighting (although not complete darkness). First of all, you will wish to observe your children as they try the mindful activities. Also some children are scared of the dark. I would suggest drawing the curtains and using a lamp or two (or candles if you can burn them safely) to give a soft, relaxing light.

One of the schools I worked with used lava lamps and projector lights on the ceiling. You may think that lighting doesn't matter if children have their eyes closed, but it does. We all gather information about our world when our eyes are open, so as we prepare to relax and meditate, it helps if the environment feels relaxing. You can also involve children in designing their own meditation space, perhaps in a corner of a room. If you are teaching meditation during the day and it's a sunny day (I'm going to contradict myself here), the sunshine coming in through the window will also create a pleasant, but different feeling.

Remember, some sessions can take place outdoors too. Just choose the environment that feels right for you and your child.

Using sound

No one lives in a vacuum so we usually have to cope with noise wherever we go. We can use noise to help with meditation, rather than hinder it.

Sound can actually become part of the meditation as you guide your children to become aware of sounds they perhaps hadn't noticed before. This approach helps them to stay in the moment and is a wonderful meditation technique for helping them to focus, concentrate and be aware.

There are certain meditations that lend themselves to silence or natural sounds, for example if you are meditating outside. You can use the sounds of nature or even the sounds of cars and traffic in your meditation, guiding children to tune into the sense of hearing and then notice when it is quieter (see p.60).

I sometimes use little Tibetan bells or singing bowls in a meditation. I ring them three times at the beginning – to signal the start of the meditation and help children to focus – and three times at the end – to help children come back into a more alert state. If you have some relaxing music that you can play then have this playing in the background. Try to dedicate the music you play to this meditation practice so that your child can differentiate between when it's meditation time and when it isn't. Ensure that the music isn't so loud that you have to speak really loudly or shout to them during meditation – it defeats the purpose!

I'm quite fussy about the music I use. Usually when I find a composer I like I buy most of their music as it suits the meditation experience. Musical taste is very personal and if you're not sure about what to use then opt for silence or ask your children to choose from a selection of soothing music.

Music can have an influence on the atmosphere you want to create. If you want to create a lighter atmosphere, for example if the child has been upset, then use light music, such as harp or piano instrumentals. If you need to calm a hyperactive child, using music with a slow rhythmical drumbeat can be effective. Use your common sense. I've listed a selection of music I use in the 'Resources' section and, where possible, indicated when I would use different types of music to create different experiences (see p.149). Using classical music can also be an option, provided it's relaxing and not stimulating. You can choose to play music for the whole of the meditation or only part of it. Remember that silence can be very calming too.

Whilst working with some children on the autistic spectrum, I've noticed that recordings of singing bowls can be very effective in helping them feel calmer. The different tones of the singing bowls have vibrations that resonate with children's energy, and in some cases help them to feel calmer. It can be very therapeutic to play them in the background any time a calming influence is needed, and feel free to try this type of sound with children who are not on the autistic spectrum (see p.149 for recommendations).

With teenagers, I sometimes find it is best not to use music. Music is so personal to that age group and they are critical of anything that doesn't fit in with their music 'scene'. Rather than add a distraction to their thoughts, like 'this music is rubbish', I generally avoid playing music, apart from occasionally using singing bowls.

Using smell

As a trained aromatherapist I know that certain aromas can affect the nervous system to provide a sense of relaxation. However, a child's respiratory system is still developing so it's important to use aromatherapy oils that their developing bodies can cope with. Less is always more where aromatherapy oils are concerned so I would only use one drop of oil if working one-to-one and a maximum of two drops if working in a larger group. Some of the oils that help relaxation and are safe to use with children are lavender (*Lavendula angustofolia*) and bergamot (*Citrus bergamia*). If you have an aromatherapy oil ceramic burner, then use this. If you don't have a ceramic burner, you can use a tissue – simply put on a drop or two and, if safe, place on the radiator to let the heat help it circulate throughout the room.

Do not over use these oils and if your child has respiratory issues or you are unsure about working with oils then consult a clinical aromatherapist for advice (see 'Resources', p.150). The Latin names for the oils (which are in brackets) are included to ensure you choose the correct type of oils, as there are several different types of lavender oil.

Some people use incense in meditation, but it can have quite a heavy scent and is perhaps not suitable for children, particularly if they have breathing difficulties like asthma.

Using touch

This is a very important sense to bring into meditation, especially for children. You can incorporate the sense of touch by providing some soft material, a cushion or a blanket for children to sit or lie on. If your children are sitting on chairs, let them rest their feet on the blanket. If their feet are bare they can pay attention to how it feels to have this soft material touching their skin. Having something tactile under their feet or body helps them to connect to the floor and ultimately to the ground, which will encourage children to be more grounded and centred, and will improve concentration (see 'Importance of Grounding' which explains why this is important in meditation. p.38). Depending on the age of your children, you could use a soft toy or teddy bear, asking them to hold and stroke it, noticing the sensation through their fingertips. Another great way to meditate with the sense of touch is using a stone or a crystal (see p.62 for examples of touch meditations).

Clutter

Try to have a space that's clean and tidy. Children are sensitive to the energy of their environment. If a room is cluttered and chaotic, this affects their energy and concentration levels. A popular space to use would be a child's bedroom. It's certainly a safe place for children to try meditation as it's their own little space in this world. If they don't have their own room, then try to have a dedicated area that they can use, and again ensure that it's clear of clutter. You can always put up a room screen to hide the clutter or make a tent using a sheet and chairs to create a homemade meditation space.

Colours

Colours have a large influence on our moods, feelings and energy. We choose the colours of clothes we want to wear and how we wish to paint our homes. We may have a favourite colour and colours that we dislike. Marketing companies know a lot about colour psychology and there is even the term 'chromodynamics' which describes how humans respond physiologically to different colours, which may, for example, stimulate or relax our focus and concentration.

Colours are highly symbolic, helping us to communicate how we feel (think about teenage goths wearing black clothes), and even to keep us safe (think about traffic lights and hazard warnings). Children's toys tend to be bright with vibrant colours as these colours appeal to them more than muted, pale colours. Brighter colours are stimulating and the colours purple and yellow are frequently used. The CBeebies logo for BBC children's TV is yellow and purple, Barney is purple, the

Teletubbies are green, purple, yellow and red, Big Bird in Sesame Street is yellow, and the McDonalds logo of golden arches is yellow. This is no accident and the marketing people who wish their products to appeal to children have chosen these colours very carefully to provoke the desired response of stimulating excitement and attraction.

Of course with meditation, we are trying to do the exact opposite – of calming children and showing them how to feel relaxed. The antidote to yellow is the colour blue, so this can be a calming colour to use, whether it's the colour of the walls or a special blanket that's used during activities. Colours that are soothing and calm are best – blues, pale colours, lilacs, creams and pinks are more energetically suited to meditation for the beginner. Please don't despair if your house is painted in bright colours, and don't let it deter you from trying. But it's something to consider if you wish to create a relaxing space.

Oddly enough, the colour red is good for meditation – particularly for those who find it hard to focus – as it has a grounding effect (see pp.38, 115). Therefore red is an effective colour for cushions and rugs to lie on to help children focus and concentrate.

This information is to provide you with a starting point and some useful tips but please remember that the environment doesn't need to be perfect. You can pick and choose those suggestions that you can most easily accommodate.

5. Energy and Meditation

My little nephew was being very fidgety and didn't want to go back to sleep and was very energetic running about, throwing things, and his mum was going crazy because he wouldn't stop. I picked him up and decided to hum 'Ommmmm'... Immediately he stopped trying to break free, looked at me, smiled and bowed his head a little even. I did it again, got him to copy me by sitting with his legs crossed and positioning his fingers in a meditation position. He watched me ... Every time I hummed 'Ommmmm', his eyes shined and he smiled ... amazing! He is only one and a half.

Uncle

It's not essential to know or understand how meditation links to energy, but it can be useful to have some level of awareness when teaching meditation.

The Eastern approach to health and well-being, where meditation is a key practice, is that we *are* energy. Not just the solid, physical energy that we touch (e.g. our bodies) but energy in the form of a vibration. There's a physical aspect to this energy (our bodies), an emotional aspect to this (our feelings) and a mental aspect to this (our thoughts). All these different aspects interact together and, when we're healthy, there is said to be a good flow of energy. Also, our energy resonates with the environment around us, and the energy of other people, as if we were sitting in a 'sea of energy'. If we compare being in nature to being in the city centre we can see how our energy is affected by our environment; if we compare being in a quiet place on our own to being in a busy shopping

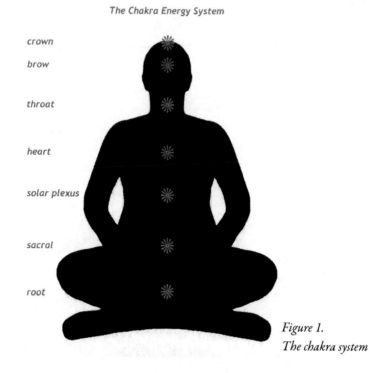

The Chakra Energy System

crown

brow

throat

heart

solar plexus

sacral

root

Figure 1.
The chakra system

centre we can see how our energy is affected by other people. This 'sea of energy' is invisible to us but exists just as much as the air we breathe.

The chakra energy system is a structure from the East, which is also now used in the West to teach this idea of energy – to help us adapt our logical minds to the idea of something as intangible as 'energy'.

According to the chakra system, when we're in good health, energy flows throughout our system and all the energy centres spin easily and gently. When we're out of balance they're either too fast or sluggish. It's suggested that when there's congestion of energy in a particular part of our system, it can manifest as a physical imbalance – ill health.

Each energy centre is said to both store the energy of experiences (physical as well as thoughts and feelings), then use this to 'filter' future experiences. If we have a negative experience that's stored in our energy, we will continue to draw on this for the future and it will affect our perception of ourselves and the world around us.

Think of your energy centres like computer discs storing data in files and retrieving it when you need it. Sometimes our files are out of date or the wrong information was entered. If we continue to use these files to interpret our lives, then our experiences can be sluggish or negative. We can choose to clear out these files if we become aware of them. In energy terms, meditation helps to identify the out-of-date files (feelings/thoughts) and clear out or update them. Meditation is a tool to help bring balance back into our energy and particularly the flow of energy through our energy centres.

Each energy centre represents a different area of our lives. For children it's exactly the same but some of the chakras are developing more than others. For example, the root chakra is at the base of the spine and connects to all things physical: your children's physical development, the physical world they live in, and the cultural beliefs they are brought up with all influence the root chakra and their physical well-being. This chakra is particularly interesting in children because it also represents how safe and grounded they feel. Many child specialists talk about the need for routine and structure. This is symbolic of the root chakra, which depends on order. Whilst the root chakra is very important in the first years of a child's life, the other energy centres are also adapting to the development of the root chakra, and each chakra in turn gets its 'fifteen minutes of fame' as the child develops into an adult.

- Root chakra – age 0–4. Physical development is the key focus.
- Sacral – age 5–7. Physical development in relation to others – family – and emotional energy starting to develop.
- Solar plexus – age 8–14. Physical development, emotional and thought development in relation to others – peers, friends, family, the world – sports, hobbies, careers.
- Heart centre – age 15–21. Physical, emotional and thought development – self-esteem, attractiveness, finding a mate, physical love.
- Throat centre – age 22–28. Less physical development and more about emotions and thoughts – relationships, marriage and children, career – choices to be made.
- Brow centre – age 29–35. Less physical development and more about emotions, thoughts – life choices of the past and present.
- Crown centre – age 36–42. Physically deteriorating – infertility, health – emotional and thought development as part of the 'big picture'.

Please be aware that this suggested energetic development pattern may vary from person to person as it is subject to the influence of external factors (environment, culture, genetics, experiences) and internal factors (thoughts, choices, feelings, emotional intelligence).

It's also useful to point out that each energy centre has a corresponding colour and simply by bringing awareness to that colour during meditation can have a particular effect on your children's energy and their ability to meditate. If you ask a child to choose the colour red, then this colour can help the child to ground their energy. The colours green and pink work with the heart centre and can help the child feel safe and nurtured. The colour blue helps to work with their throat chakra so they have a more balanced voice (or balance between listening and talking). I would avoid choosing a colour specifically for children to meditate with because *you think* this will somehow 'fix' them. Our energy is very sensitive to any form of control or manipulation and will usually react against this, whatever age we are. If you allow your children to choose their colour, you may find out which energy centre is important to them and which area of their energy is trying to come into balance. Being aware of your child's choice of colour and researching the corresponding chakra afterwards can be very informative.

Although I tend to use colour with children, you can also ask them to focus on their body as a barometer of their energy. If you ask them to place their hands on their body, either where it does or doesn't feel comfortable, you can tell which chakra is drawing most attention at that time. This is useful if children find it difficult to 'imagine'; placing their hands on their body is a good alternative as it offers a tactile approach.

The importance of grounding

When people first come to learn meditation in my classes, they often have an idea that meditation is about floating off on a nice cloud of 'nothingness', leaving the cares and worries of the day-to-day world behind. Whilst it's true that we get some relief from the challenges we face, in meditation 'speak', it's important to be 'grounded'.

Grounding your energy means ensuring that your energy is firmly tethered to the ground through your body. Think of it like a balloon tethered to the ground – the rope can only be extended if there's a firm anchor. If the rope is released then the balloon is lost and can't find its base again. In my experience, the most common signs of someone being ungrounded are that they can't focus or concentrate, they have sleep and energy issues and they are very emotional. If the person is ungrounded and sitting in a chair, they can't keep their feet flat on the ground or if lying down or sitting on the floor cross-legged, they constantly fidget. It can take some practice, but that's why it's so important to feel and sense the connection with the ground before and after any meditation practice. It allows children to feel safe when their mind is taken on a guided journey. Or it helps them to focus when they are trying to gain some control over the thousands of thoughts they think each day.

The energy centre in our system of chakras that connects to grounding is our 'root' energy centre at the base of our spine. The colour of this energy centre is red, which is often used as a colour for safety and protection: a red traffic light warns us not to go forward and thereby protects our physical safety. The colours of red, black and brown are all very grounding colours and help us to keep our energy grounded and safe. We use phrases in society like 'I stood firm', 'I can stand on my own two feet' and 'I felt like the ground had been swept from under me'. These phrases help confirm how the root centre, which connects via the legs and feet to the earth, is important to our health and well-being, and especially in meditation.

To be grounded means to focus on the ground and our connection to it. Having your feet flat on the floor is a good starting point, or if sitting cross-legged just noticing how the base of our spine touches the floor. We can then think about how the floor connects to the earth beneath us. Sometimes I use imagery whilst asking children to breathe through their feet into the ground – imagining that they have roots like a plant going down with each out-breath into the ground – getting stronger and wider and deeper. Then, when the roots have travelled firmly into the ground, I ask them to imagine breathing up the strength from the earth through these roots into their feet, to the base of their spines and into their bodies. It helps stabilise their energy and helps them to focus.

Grounding is such a useful exercise that it can be a simple meditation all on its own, or you can use it at the beginning of the meditation and at the end. When someone is 'ungrounded' they feel woozy, light-headed and unstable. It's worth also mentioning that in my experience we are more accident-prone if we are ungrounded, hence why I make sure my students are grounded at the end of a meditation class before they get into their cars to drive home!

If at the end of a meditation you and your child feel ungrounded then just tap your feet on the floor. I always encourage people who have been meditating to move slowly at first and stretch arms, legs and hands to 'feel' their body again.

Further on in this book I talk about how being aware of the energy centres can be very useful in relating to issues like ADHD (see Chapter 13) and autism (see Chapter 14) or how to work if your child can't 'imagine' a colour (see case study p.123). I also give tips for showing your children how to ground their energy (see p.115–121). It's very important for you, the teacher, to be grounded when trying to show children meditation as it helps you to feel calm and centred.

Energy in groups and self-meditation

When we practise meditation alone, we are working with our own energy and it can often feel a little bit challenging. However when we meditate in a group, the group energy blends together and this can make the meditation experience seem easier.

If you're helping your child to meditate, your energy will connect. If you're teaching one, two or more children together, you form a group, which can help the meditation flow more easily. Experience has taught me that for beginners, a group is a very supportive environment in which to learn meditation. The energy of the group is shared, with each person giving and receiving support through their energy.

Here is a very simple explanation. Let's compare our energy to having our own dimmer switch that connects to our internal light, which we can turn up or down. When we meditate it's like turning the dimmer switch up and our own energy expands, becoming brighter and stronger. Each person in a group is turning up their own internal light and hence expanding their energy. As the light expands more and more, the space becomes brighter. Our light (energy) does not fight for space but shares the space and collectively makes the 'group light' brighter. This sharing does not come about through our will power – it happens because we let go, relax and allow our energy to connect more with the energy of the environment. So our energy receives from others and also gives to others and we find that we can 'sit' in the meditation space more easily as we are working within a collective energy field rather than simply our own. It's like sharing the air that we breathe. We don't fight for it but simply share it with each other and with nature around us.

Energy centres for teaching meditation

The role of your own energy centres is important in teaching meditation.

The solar plexus – this energy centre is concerned with doing things right and being right. It holds the energy of control and self-esteem. It is heavily involved in how we judge ourselves through the eyes of others and how we judge others. If you're trying to make your children meditate or have specific ideas about how they should behave in meditation, then the solar plexus is involved. Being aware of this centre and relaxing it with the breath (breathing in and out of the area) can help you to let go of any judging thoughts whilst you are teaching meditation.

The heart centre – this energy centre is important in helping you to let go and connect with your children in an unconditional way. Allowing them to just 'be'. It holds the energy of unconditional love and if we teach with the wisdom of the heart centre then we are not trying to control but are simply observing the meditation with love. Once the solar plexus is relaxed, you can focus on the heart energy centre with your breath to help you relax and let go as you teach meditation.

The root centre – this energy centre helps you to stay calm, focused and centred whilst you show children how to meditate. Often adults can be a little bit nervous the first time they try to teach children meditation. If you follow the tips on grounding, just as you encourage your children to be grounded, you will find that you're calmer and teaching meditation will be much more enjoyable for you.

6. Starting and Finishing Meditations

I work as a special needs teaching assistant in quite a challenging primary school. Last year we introduced guided meditation sessions to a Year Six class after play and dinner times. The children responded well and most noticeable was the calmness about them when they moved around the room.

Teacher

Naturally with every meditation there is a starting point, a middle point and an end point. How long each of these phases lasts depends on the age of your child and how much time you have to meditate.

The starting point is to bring focus and concentration to the meditation. I usually use the breath for all age groups (it has to be more tactile with younger children) as this is the anchor point for everyone. Wherever you go, you breathe. Once you have focused on the breath, I encourage you to help your child relax – especially if the meditation is a longer session.

Then there is the middle section – what are you going to do? Is it a sound meditation or using another sense? Are you guiding children using words and phrases? Are you taking them on a guided and peaceful journey? How long you and your child wish to meditate can determine what you do here.

Finally there is the end section – bringing children's awareness back to the here and now so that when they open their eyes they feel grounded, safe and peaceful. This is also an excellent opportunity to chat about what children experienced. Encourage them to draw or write it down – keeping a journal of their meditations.

Now let me expand a little further on the starting and finishing sections so you can see how a meditation can develop.

Starting a meditation

Hopefully you have created a suitable environment (see Chapter 4). Now it's time to start the meditation and I usually do this with the breath, followed by relaxation.

The breath

Using the breath is the first stepping-stone to taking children's awareness into a state of meditation and peacefulness. Another benefit of using the breath as a focal point is that it's always there no matter where they go. No special equipment is needed, just a little bit of guidance suitable to their age and ability. The more they practise this, the more children learn that they have this 'anchor' and can switch their awareness to it whenever they need to. You could say that the breath is your child's 'calm button'!

Teaching children to focus on the breath is a quick way to get them to pay attention to the here and now. It sounds easy, but the challenge arises in keeping the attention on the breath as the mind tends to wander. However, using the breath to help with their initial focus, and to come back to it throughout the meditation if the mind wanders or there is a disruption, makes it a very useful tool. And when we start to notice the breath (even if it is really fast or shallow to being with), it usually starts to come into balance and will help your child relax.

There are meditations which are all about the breath. However, for children (and particularly small children), the breath is not interesting enough to hold their attention for long periods of time. As they grow older they can focus on the breath for longer.

Common phrases I use to start meditations are: 'Notice your thoughts and blow them away' and 'Notice your breath'. You may also have to gently guide children to keep themselves connected to the ground if they are sitting and they start to lift their feet: 'Feel the ground under the soles of your feet'. You may wish to spend 1–5 minutes just doing this, but remember it depends on age and ability so go with what feels right.

It might help to try any of the following suggestions:

NOTICING THE BREATH (AGE 6 AND UNDER)

When working with younger children it can be a little bit more challenging to notice the breath, so I would usually use a tactile approach. You could get them to pay attention to the breath first of all by touching their nose. Then you could ask them to hold their hands in front of their nose with their mouth slightly open so they can feel the warmth of the breath on their hands as they breathe out and the coolness as they breathe in.

With a younger age group you usually have to give them more instruction on how to use their senses. So you could also ask them to listen to their breath too. Encourage them to notice the sound of their breath as they breathe in and out through their mouth, making an 'ahhhh' sound. This helps them focus on what you're asking them to do. You could get them to be silent on the in-breath and say the word 'whoosh' or 'laaaa' on the out-breath – or it could be their favourite word.

Here are some examples to help younger children focus on the breath:

Where you read the word 'pause' be silent for 1–2 breaths before moving on to the next step.

Put your hands in front of your face.
Palms are facing your nose.
Notice that when you breathe out through your mouth, the air touches your hands. *(pause)*
Notice each breath touching your hands.
Let go of your thoughts.
Just notice the warm air of your breath on your hands. *(pause)*
Now notice how cool it feels on your hands when you breathe in.
Warm when you breathe out.
Cool when you breathe in.
Warm when you breathe out.
Cool when you breathe in.
This time, blow your thoughts away as you breathe out.

Blow your thoughts into your hands as you breathe out. *(pause)*
Each time you breathe into your hands, you feel lighter inside.
Each time you breathe into your hands, you feel happier inside.
Each time you breathe into your hands, you feel softer inside.
  (pause)

You can use words like peaceful, calmer, smoother – just choose the words they will understand.

Put your hands down but pay attention to your breath still going
  in and out. *(pause)*
Notice how you feel inside.
Smile as you breath in and out – notice how that feels. *(pause)*

At this point they can stop, or for a longer session take them into relaxation and meditation.

If your children are a bit older and can hold their attention on their breath then miss out having their hands in front of their faces. Get them to move their focus to the tips of their noses to notice the breath as it moves in and out – each out-breath lets them feel more relaxed and lighter. The in-breath is 'cool' and the out-breath is 'warm'. You can ask them to 'shake' out all the thoughts they breathed into their hands as if they are helping to get rid of any worrying thoughts.

COUNTING THE BREATH (AGE 7+)

Here you ask children to focus on the breath by counting it. Counting the breath gives their logical part of the brain something to focus on. It's especially good for children who like numbers. The intention of this practice is not to rush the counting and reach a high number but to use the counting to level or slow down the breath. Whatever number your children reach does not matter. They are counting silently to themselves and seeing how long they can stretch each number. After they have practised this for a few breaths, you can ask them to hold their breath (after the in-breath for the count of 1) then to count the breath slowly as they breathe out. If they have been breathing very quickly, you may find that your child's breath starts to rebalance and slow down. Here is an example:

Where you read the word 'pause' be silent for 1–2 breaths before moving on to the next step.

When you breathe in through your nose, start counting your breath slowly *(silently)*.
1................ 2.................
Let go of your out-breath *(through your mouth)*.
Count your in-breath again *(silently)*.
1................ 2.................
Let go of your out-breath *(through your mouth)*.
Now this time count your in-breath *(silently)* then count your out-breath slowly.
Repeat this again. *You may need to guide them again.*

After several repetitions of those steps you can ask:

Is the in-breath number the same as the out-breath number? *(pause)*
Are the numbers different? *(pause)*
Okay – now stop counting and just notice your in- and out-breaths for a few breaths.
This time after you breathe in, hold your breath for a count of 1 then breathe out slowly.
Repeat this a few more times, trying to help the out-breath slow down. *(pause)*

Imagery can be used for the out-breath, such as blowing out a candle or blowing into a balloon, if this helps with concentration.

Noticing the breath (age 12+)

If you're teaching older children, using the breath is a good starting point, as they can usually take their attention to their breath quite easily with a simple instruction. Let me give you an example:

Where you read the word 'pause', continue to practise that step for 2–3 breaths.

Take your attention to your nose.
Notice your breath moving in and out. *(pause)*
Now notice its rhythm.
Just be curious and let go with each out-breath. *(pause)*
Now notice its pace.
Now notice its depth. *(pause)*
And now notice the gentle movement of your chest as the breath moves in... then out... *(pause)*

CHEST AND TUMMY BREATH (ALL AGES)

Adapt the language to suit the age group. Ask children to pay attention to their breath for several breaths as you pause before moving on to the next sentence.

Put your hands on your chest.
Notice when you breathe in your chest moves up.
Notice when you breathe out your chest moves down. *(pause)*
Notice when you breathe in your hands and chest move.
Notice when you breathe out your hands and chest move.
Let go of your thoughts. *(pause)*
Breathe in a little more air and notice your hands go higher.
Breathe out a little more air and notice your hands go lower. *(pause)*
Notice how your chest fills with air like a balloon.
Notice how your chest falls slowly like letting air out of a balloon.
Let go of your thoughts. *(pause)*
Take your hands down now to your belly button.
Let your hands rest on your tummy.
Notice when you breathe in your hands go up, your tummy gently rises.
Notice as you breathe out your hands move down, your tummy falls. *(pause)*

Notice each breath your hands going up, then down.
Notice each breath your tummy going up, then down.
Let go of your thoughts. *(pause)*
Breathe in a little more air and notice your hands go higher.
Breathe out a little more air and notice your hands go lower.
  (pause)
Just notice how your tummy fills with air like a balloon.
Notice how your tummy falls slowly like letting air out of a
  balloon.
Let go of your thoughts. *(pause)*
Each time you breathe out you feel calmer inside.
Each time you breathe out you feel quieter inside. *(pause)*
Each time you breathe out you feel safer inside.

*You can use words like peaceful, calmer, smoother – just choose the
words they will understand.*

Notice how you feel inside.
Smile and notice how you feel inside.

At this point you can end here or carry on into a longer meditation.

Relaxation

It sounds like simple common sense, however it's important to stress
that both you and your child should be in relaxed positions when
trying to meditate. Children are usually very receptive to relaxation
methods (more so than adults!), although they do need some gentle
encouragement at the start to get them 'in the mood' to try meditation.
Children seem to let go and relax much more easily and are usually
much more willing to work with their imagination than adults, who
tend to let their logical minds get in the way.

Being relaxed allows children to gently rest their attention on the
meditation practice, helping them to enjoy and focus on the present
moment. PMR, or Progressive Muscle Relaxation, is a useful first step.

This involves taking children's attention through each part of their bodies, step by step, encouraging their bodies to relax and let go of any tension. For example, you could start by focusing on their feet, tensing them for a few seconds then letting them relax. Tense and relax, tense and relax. You can decide to start at the head and work down or the feet and work up concentrating on each part of their bodies (feet, legs, hips, tummy, chest, arms, hands, shoulders and face) with the gentle intention of letting that part start to relax as they let go. Ask them to tense and relax the part of the body they are focusing on, then combine this with the in- and out-breath. So, for example, once they have been tensing their feet and letting them relax, I then ask them to breathe in when they tense and breathe out when they relax. Here is an example of a relaxation script, which you can adapt to suit children of all ages:

RELAXATION

This relaxation is based on the child sitting but you can change the words to suit if they are lying on the floor or in their bed.

Put your feet on the ground so that they are flat (*or if cross-legged feel the bottom of your spine touching the floor*).

Imagine you have a string attached to the top of your head and it is being gently pulled up to the sky – stretching your back and neck long like a giraffe.

Then imagine the string becoming loose and your head gently relaxes on top of your neck.

Let your hands rest in your lap facing up.

We are going to start some relaxation from the top and work down.

First of all smile – notice the feeling in your face and how your face feels.

Then frown – notice how it feels different.

Repeat last 2 sentences a few times.

Now make a funny face – all the muscles in your face go tight.

Then let go and feel your muscles go soft.

Repeat last 2 sentences a few times.

Notice the difference when your muscles feel tight and muscles feel soft.

Let your face relax. *(pause)*

Now go to your shoulders.

Lift them up towards your ears as if your shoulders and ears can touch.

Then let them drop gently back down.

Repeat last 2 sentences a few times.

Do this again – slower this time.

Notice the difference when the muscles feel tight and the muscles feel soft. *(pause)*

Now go to your arms – stretch out your arms.

Let them go soft and floppy.

Repeat last 2 sentences a few times.

Just tense one arm then let it go soft and floppy.

Then tense the other arm then let it go soft and floppy. *(pause)*

Now go to your hands – close your hand and make the shape of a rock.

Then open your hands and fingers so they look like a star.

Rocks

Stars

Repeat last 2 sentences a few times. (pause)

Now go to your tummy – push your tummy out.

Then relax.

Then do it again – hold – then relax.

Imagine you have a balloon in your tummy as you push it out.

Then imagine all the air in the balloon escapes as you relax.

Do this again – slower this time – so you can notice the difference when the muscles feel tight and muscles feel soft. *(pause)*

Now go to your legs – tighten your legs as if they were planks of wood – let them relax as if they were feathers.

Planks of wood

Feathers

Planks of wood

Feathers *(pause)*

Now go to your feet – curl your toes as if they are little mice hiding in a mouse hole.

Then stretch out your toes as if the mouse has popped out of its
  mouse hole.
Repeat last 2 sentences a few times.
Do this again – slower this time – so you can notice the difference
  when the muscles feel tight and muscles feel soft.

*Combining imagery with relaxation can make it easier for children
to understand what you are asking them to do and make it more fun.
This example is suited to younger children so use appropriate words
and imagery for your child's age.*

If your children are hyperactive or have pain in their bodies then you
may have to spend more time guiding them through the relaxation stage.
Let them find their way gradually. A top tip is for them to acknowledge
their pain and try to breath into that area or imagine they are breathing
the pain into their chest (heart centre). In terms of energy, this can help
lessen the sensation of the pain during that time.

If you and your children are just trying a short 1-minute meditation,
the relaxation part can be short or non-existent (e.g. if you are doing
a 1-minute breath meditation). If you are intending to take them on a
longer guided meditation, it's useful to help them relax first.

Finishing the meditation

If you have taken children on a longer meditation (e.g. breath, relaxation
then a guided journey), it's important to bring the meditation to an end.

Just as you started with the breath, it's a great idea to finish with
the breath by simply asking them to notice it. If they have been really
relaxed in their meditation you may wish to give them a few moments
to come round.

Then using the breath you can guide them into their bodies –
noticing how their bodies receive and release the breath. You can ask
children to wiggle their toes, stretch their legs, stretch their arms up
and wiggle their fingers. All of this helps them to come back fully into
their bodies.

If your children have been doing an activity about staying in the present (e.g. noticing sound or taste) they won't need too much time to come back. However it's worth spending a few moments just asking them to notice how calm they feel inside. This feeling is a memory that our children can tap into when they need to access that quiet space within.

Sharing

I always think it's worth taking a few moments to see how your children felt during the meditation. What did they remember, feel or see? Ask them to write or draw their experiences. Having their own journals is a great idea as this helps them to remember the experiences and process their thoughts and feelings. Even if you have a big group, make time for this. I learned this lesson when teaching a group in school. At the end of the meditation I asked each child what colours they saw and what they felt. The last boy to speak seemed a little timid but he told me what he saw and felt. Afterwards the head teacher was amazed as she told me that due to this boy's difficult background he never, ever spoke. It was a humbling moment for me.

7. Different Types of Meditation

I get my son to listen to the rain falling outside the window, or the wind blowing through the trees. He jokes around with me about it, but I notice a massive and immediate change in his mood.

Parent

When you think of using meditation techniques with children, perhaps you thought you would all be seated on the floor, cross-legged in a typical meditation pose in complete silence? This is a common perception of meditation and as the adult you may be thinking, 'How in the world will I get my children to do this?'

Since most adults find learning meditation challenging, they think it must be the same for children. Yes children have lots of energy and are bursting with life as they run around, jumping and shouting, however let me assure you that they are also capable of quietness and stillness. This chapter aims to expand your perception of what meditation is by exploring a range of mindful activities and showing you how your children can experience and enjoy meditation.

Being in the moment – mindfulness

One aspect of meditation is simply about being in the moment. It is about asking children to pay attention to how they feel, what they are thinking and how their body feels in this moment. It sounds simple (and it is) so it's a good starting point, whatever age your children are.

One approach is referred to as 'living in the moment with the breath'. This means showing your children how to be completely aware of their breath *in this very moment* – of being 'mindful' in this moment. So it's the opposite of thinking about the moment that has passed or the moment yet to come. It also means not judging the moment but simply noticing it. As I have already mentioned, when I teach meditation, I ask children and adults to focus on their breath because your breath is with you in every moment – at home, school, in the park – so children can use it at any point in their day. (Don't forget how much this can benefit you too – at the bus stop, waiting in the supermarket queue, stuck in a traffic jam...) What usually happens with anyone who learns meditation with the breath is that you get bored or distracted by thoughts. Thoughts enter your head and before you know it you've forgotten to focus on your breath. Instead, you become distracted by your thoughts. Let me give you an example:

Teacher: 'Focus on the breath.'
Teacher: 'Follow the breath into your body.'
You: Feel pain in your shoulder.
Your thought: 'Oh I've got a sore shoulder...'
Your thought: 'I must try to relax it more...'
Your thought: 'Well, I've been working a lot on the pc...'
Your thought: 'Maybe I should change the height of my chair at work...'
Your thought: 'I could book in for a massage, that would help...'
Your thought: 'I wonder when I could book that in...'
Your thought: 'I wonder how much it will cost...'
Your thought: 'Not sure I can afford it this month...'
Your thought: 'Must remember to pay that bill...'
Teacher: 'Focus on the breath and let go of any thoughts.'
Your thought: 'Oh no! I must get back to my breath...'

Through this short example, you can see how your train of thought takes you away from your breath. At this point when I'm teaching, I usually say to students, 'Acknowledge your thoughts and let them go and come back to the breath' and they realise what's happened. When you're teaching children meditation you can say something similar: 'Notice your breath now' so they know to come back to the breath.

With practice, what eventually happens is that we learn to let go of the thoughts more easily and to focus on the breath for longer. This is a really useful technique for teenagers to help them cope with exam stress and nerves. For younger children I would make it more interactive (see p.44). This is a good practice to try with children as it can be introduced regularly and at any point in the day. It can almost become a regular exercise or game of noticing the breath. Eventually, your children can practise by themselves without your help. This method is very good for helping children to learn how to focus and concentrate for longer periods of time and not be so easily distracted.

Whether adult, teenager or child, if they can focus for only one breath, this is a good start. Gradually, they will build up the ability to focus and be aware of more and more breaths.

This approach is a key part of mindfulness meditation practice, which is becoming increasingly popular with psychologists and those in mental health care; mindfulness is a key part of many Buddhist practices. Mindfulness encourages you to be aware of your mind, your thoughts and your breath. The intention is about letting your awareness stay in the moment so that you can bring meditation into ordinary life.

To give you a flavour of what this feels like, you can try this simple exercise:

BEING IN THE MOMENT

Where you read the word 'pause', continue to practise that step for 2–3 breaths.

As you read this take your attention to your breath. To do this, take your attention to the tip of your nose and just be aware of your breath. *(pause)*

Become aware of how your breath moves in and out of your body. Is your mouth involved? Or are you breathing in and out of your nose? *(pause)*

Keep noticing your breath and be aware of how deep or shallow it is. Notice if you are judging your breath for how shallow or short it is. If you are, let go of these judging thoughts and just watch or feel your breath. *(pause)*

Keep noticing your breath and be aware of the pace of your breath – is it fast or slow or somewhere in between? *(pause)*

Let go of trying to change your breath and just simply feel it. *(pause)*

Now can you feel how your breath moves into your chest? Do you notice the rise and fall of your chest as you breathe in, then out? *(pause)*

Notice your thoughts – are you feeling anxious or relaxed with this breath? *(pause)*

Notice your thoughts as they come up, but let them go and just return to the breath. Follow the in- and the out-breath. *(pause)*

Take your attention to your body – does it feel tight and tense or relaxed? *(pause)*

Let go of your thoughts and just be curious about how your body feels. *(pause)*

Change your posture if you wish to make it more comfortable then come back to the breath.

When you breathe in, let that breath flow into your body where it is tense and as you breathe out just mentally say the word 'relax'. Keep doing this with each breath and just watch. *(pause)*

Be aware of feelings and thoughts as they come up but let them go. Just allow that breath to come into your body and let the body relax on the out-breath – be curious and watch. *(pause)*

Congratulations! You have just taken part in a meditation (perhaps your first). How do you feel? Was it difficult or easy? Was your mind full of thoughts? Did you feel anxious or good? Did your body feel tense or release any of the tension? Whatever you experienced, this is meditation. Even if you think 'oh my mind was too busy' or 'I was uncomfortable' this is still meditation. Buddhists say that when we notice the 'monkey chatter' of the mind, we are taking our first step in meditation. Don't worry about how busy your mind was, as this is you becoming aware of the mind and its chatter. If you were experiencing the activity and not thinking about day-to-day thoughts then you were 'in the moment'.

The above meditation can be adapted to suit different ages of children and their range of attention spans (see Chapter 10). However it has given you an opportunity to try an aspect of meditation that was not about sitting cross-legged but simply in your chair during everyday life.

ON THE SPOT MEDITATIONS

This is where you simply spend a moment meditating 'on the spot' – for no longer than a minute. You and the children can be seated or standing.

Eyes closed (*if open then look at the ground – soft gaze*).
Take your attention to your nose.
Notice your breath.
In
Out
In
Out
Is it fast or slow? (*pause*)
How does your body feel? (*pause*)
Imagine each time you breathe out your body feels calmer and softer like a feather.
Calmer and softer (*pause*)
Calmer and softer
Where are you? (*pause*)
What can you hear? (*pause*)
What are your feet touching? (*pause*)
What are your hands touching? (*pause*)
Are your fingers touching? (*pause*)
Take a deep breath in.
Breathe out and open your eyes.

Using day-to-day activities

Students in my classes are often surprised when I talk about the 'cup of tea' meditation or the 'shower' meditation. In other words trying to meditate as you do normal stuff! If, like me, you are busy, you're more likely to try something that you can easily fit into your routine.

I remember listening to a Buddhist talk many years ago, which encouraged the audience to slow down and practise meditation whilst doing ordinary things, like eating or washing dishes. At this time in my life I was so stressed, I felt I would be incredibly frustrated trying to slow down to this snail's pace. However, I persevered and I have since learned that it's a useful, practical approach. Here's an example:

Cup of tea meditation

This meditation is for you to try (as an adult) where you simply spend a moment meditating whilst making and drinking a cup of tea. These few moments spent noticing sounds and other senses allow you some respite from your day-to-day thoughts and feelings.

Take your attention to your nose.
Notice your breath.
In
Out
In
Out
Now walk to the kitchen and notice your footsteps on the floor – notice the sense of touch and the sounds of your footsteps.
Lift the kettle to the sink and feel the warmth/coolness of the handle.
Notice its weight in your hand.
Run the water and hear the sounds of it running.
Notice the sounds change as you fill the kettle (and notice the weight of the kettle getting heavier).
Plug the kettle in to boil and notice the sounds it makes.
Hear the sounds you make as you take a cup and spoon and place your teabag in the cup.
Feel the coolness of the spoon in your hand.
Go to the fridge door and hear it opening and feel the cool air surround you.
Feel the cool milk in your hand.
Listen to the kettle boil and feel the heat from it.

> Make the cup of tea whilst listening to sounds and feeling warmth or coolness.
>
> Lift the tea to your lips and feel the warmth of the steam on your face.
>
> Feel and taste the liquid as you drink your tea.

It will be interesting for you to discover new meditation activities with your children. It might be that you do this as you're walking, in the park, before bedtime, in the bath... there are lots of choices. If you can do this *and* make the time to find 10–15 minutes to do seated meditation – brilliant! But you may not have that time. Find a way that suits you, your lifestyle and the personalities of you and your children. Here are some suggestions of activities that could become meditations in your daily routine. I have suggested the senses you might ask your children to focus on as they do these activities. You can refer to the earlier section on meditating using the breath (p.43) and the following section on meditating using the senses (p.60) for explanations and examples on how to guide your children.

- Brushing teeth – taste, touch, sound
- Brushing hair – sound, touch
- Having a bath or shower – touch, sound (include towel drying in this)
- Eating fruit – taste, sound, smell, touch (see example on p.63)
- Walking – sound, touch, counting steps, breath, colours, smell
- Eating dinner – smell, taste, sound (as they eat), energy in food (sun, rain, journey to table)
- Homework – breath, grounded (feet or spine on ground)
- Walking the dog – breath, touch (feet on ground), sound (dog panting), tension on leash
- Brushing or petting animal – touch (softness of their coat, warmth), sound (brushing or purring)
- Bedtime – touch, breath

Top tip: using an 'on the spot' 1-minute meditation in any of these situations is a useful way to introduce this to your child.

Using the physical senses

Using your senses is one style of meditation. The five physical senses help children to be aware of the 'here and now' and the world around them. It could simply be paying attention to their posture. As you read this chapter, start to notice your own posture – notice if it's slightly crooked, or the sensation of touch whilst your body is standing, sitting or resting. As you become aware of your body and the sensation of touch, you might decide to relax or change your position so that your posture feels better. Simply by noticing your body you can let go of tension that you are subliminally holding on to.

Another of the senses that can be used successfully is listening to sound. We can encourage our children to listen with awareness and without judging and labelling sounds – just noticing them. Our world is very noisy and usually we pay no attention to the sounds in our environment; these external sounds are like white noise surrounding us. We can selectively notice sound if we choose to, like noticing bird song or the sound of your steps as you're walking, and immediately we take our awareness away from our thoughts and towards the moment.

You could use the sense of smell. If you and your children are outside in a garden or park, then you will start to notice the subtle smells of the grass, flowers and shrubs once you start to tune into them during meditation.

You can also use the sense of sight with more awareness. As humans we take in most of our information through our eyes, but we can pay more attention to our environment, such as noticing colours, shapes or patterns. Or we can pay attention to something in our world – flowers, stones or a picture – with more awareness. Meditation is about being in a state of relaxed awareness. It allows us to observe the world but with wonder and curiosity, not judgement.

We can also use the senses of touch and taste.

If you show your children how to use their senses to meditate, they can use the environment around them to help. This helps to avoid distractions. If there is an unexpected noise, you can incorporate it into the meditation. I find that children are very good at relaxing in a noisy environment as they learn to shut it out when they're at school. It's we adults who get really annoyed with noisy distractions!

Focus meditation – sound

Remember to pause for a few breaths (as indicated).

When you breathe out – imagine you are breathing out of your ears.

Notice the space around your ears – feel it – think about it – imagine it. *(pause)*

In that space around your ears – do you notice any sound? *(pause)*

Just notice any sounds coming into your ears.

Or maybe it is quiet in that space? *(pause)*

Can you hear your breath? *(pause)*

Notice when there is a sound and when it is quiet. *(pause)*

When you breathe out – imagine the space all around you in this room – feel it – think it – imagine it. *(pause)*

In that space all around the room – do you notice any sound?

Just notice the sound – then let go of the sound. *(pause)*

Do you notice how it feels different when there is sound and when it is quiet? *(pause)*

Can you hear my voice moving towards you? Can you hear the sound of my voice? *(pause)*

When you breathe out – imagine the space outside this room– feel it – think it – imagine it.

In that space outside – do you notice any sound? *(pause)*

Just notice it then let it go.

Do you notice any different sounds? Notice them one by one – let them go. *(pause)*

Do you notice how it feels different when there is sound and when it is quiet? *(pause)*

Follow the sounds – how far do they go? *(pause)*

When you breathe out – come back and start to imagine the space all around you in this room.

Notice the sounds in this room. *(pause)*

Notice my voice. Just notice the sound – then let go. *(pause)*

When you breathe out – imagine that space around your ears.

Notice that space – any sound? *(pause)*

Notice your breath. *(pause)*
Breathe out and gently open your eyes.

Focus meditation – touch

You can use a stone or crystal for this meditation.

Hold a stone in the palm of one hand – eyes open.
Look at the stone and notice any patterns or colours. *(pause)*
Close your eyes.
Notice how heavy the stone feels. *(pause)*
Gently stroke the stone with your fingertips. Does it feel rough? Does it feel smooth? How does it feel? *(pause)*
Feel the shape of the stone with your fingers – stroke your fingers around the stone. Is it big? Is it small? How does it feel? *(pause)*
Hold the stone in both hands. Does it feel warm? Does it feel cool? How does it feel? *(pause)*
Think about the ground that the stone came from – it came from the earth – the earth beneath you.
Think how strong that stone is – it came from the earth. *(pause)*
Can you imagine the part of the earth the stone came from?
How deep down was the stone in the earth? *(pause)*
Can you imagine that stone in the earth?
Can you imagine how safe that stone feels? *(pause)*
Then repeat the above questions as appropriate to get them to sense their stones. Remember to pause after questions to give them time to respond to the question.
Imagine each time you breathe in you are breathing in the energy of the stone.
Breathing in the strength of the stone. *(pause)*
Breathing in the feeling of the stone. *(pause)*
Feeling safe every time you breathe in – feel this stone in your hands. *(pause)*

When you are ready, start to trace your fingers around the stone –
feeling the shape, surface. *(pause)*
When you are ready – open your eyes and notice how you feel
inside.

FOCUS MEDITATION – TASTE

Taste can become a meditation practice in itself. Give your children a
banana or piece of apple or a raisin and teach them how to focus on
it. Guide them through this as a meditation, asking them first of all to
smell it (maybe with their eyes open, then eyes closed), then ask them
to notice the sensation and texture of the skin and ask them to notice
how heavy it feels. Then when they take a bite, ask them to notice the
flavour, its sweetness or saltiness, or whether if feels warm or cool. Below
is an example:

FOCUS MEDITATION – MANY SENSES

Use an apple or piece of apple, or any piece of fruit that they like.

Hold the apple in your hand – eyes open.
See the apple – is it large or small – notice the colour – does it
change around the apple? *(pause)*
Close your eyes.
Hold the apple up to your nose. How does it smell? *(pause)*
Feel the apple in your hand. Is it soft or hard? Is it cool or warm?
(pause)
Trace your fingers over the apple. Is it smooth or rough?
Can you feel and see through your fingers? *(pause)*
Does the apple feel big or small? How does it feel? *(pause)*
Hold the apple in your lap – and imagine all the sunshine that
helped this apple to grow.
Can you feel the sunshine in this apple?
How does the sunshine feel? *(pause)*

Imagine all the rain in this apple that helped it to grow.

Can you imagine the rain?

How does the rain feel? *(pause)*

Imagine the tree that the apple came from – can you imagine the tree?

How tall is the tree?

How does that tree feel? *(pause)*

Can you imagine the earth beneath the tree? *(pause)*

Hold the apple to your nose – can you smell it?

How does it smell? *(pause)*

Now bite into the apple – how does it taste? Cool? Sweet? *(pause)*

Listen to the noise you make as you eat this apple. *(pause)*

Take your time – be curious about this apple and how it feels to be eating it.

After you have finished eating, breathe in and then breathe out and gently open your eyes.

Visualisation (guiding the imagination)

Logic will get you from A to Z; imagination will get you everywhere.

Albert Einstein

This type of practice involves guiding your child's imagination. Rather like following a story, you are leading children with words to help their imagination create a path to a place of peacefulness. It can also be a useful approach in helping your children offload mental or emotional worries simply by using imagery. In this peaceful place you can help them imagine whatever they need to feel relaxed, safe and calm.

Although the journey is an imaginary one, children's bodies don't realise this so they will behave as if they are actually in this peaceful place. In my adult meditation classes I have shown students that, by using their imagination, they can create the physical response of producing more saliva in their mouth if they imagine that they are sucking on a lemon. The body thinks this is real so it responds with more saliva.

Note that the body responds with stress to negative, worrying thoughts (see Chapter 2), so the opportunity to imagine a restful, safe place helps children to let go of their stress.

The word 'visualisation' is slightly misleading as it suggests that when you visualise, your children only see images in 'their mind's eye'. Some children's imaginations may not be very visual. Ask children to imagine their favourite toy – do they see the colours/detail? They may be kinaesthetic or auditory, where they sense more strongly through touch or sound. So instead of them seeing the toy they might imagine feeling it in their hands or hearing the noises it makes. When using visualisation in a meditation you might encourage your child to smell the grass instead of, or as well as, seeing it, or to hear the birds singing. It's useful to explore all the senses if possible – sight, sound, smell, taste and touch. Here is an example:

SEASIDE VISUALISATION

Use this after breath and relaxation steps.

Imagine there is a door in front of you – is it a big door or a small door? *(pause)*
Imagine that there is a beautiful handle on this door – it turns easily.
And when you go through the door you are outside and standing on a beach.
Imagine the sun in the sky – a clear blue sky – you can feel the warm sun on your skin.
How do you feel? *(pause)*
Imagine that there is a breeze – the wind tickles your skin.
Imagine the sand under your feet – it is soft and warm – heated up by the sun – start to walk across the sand. *(pause)*
Imagine the sounds of the birds – you can hear them calling to each other – flying in the sky.
Imagine the sounds of the waves – you can hear the waves moving towards you – moving away – back into the sea. *(pause)*
Stop somewhere on the beach and watch the waves – moving towards you – and away – lots of white froth on the top of each

wave – watch the wave get bigger then crash down onto the seashore.

You see a seashell on the ground – it is a beautiful colour – shining in the sun.

Imagine running your fingers over the seashell.

Pick it up – how does it feel? *(pause)*

Hold the seashell to your ear – you can hear the sounds of the sea again but they are louder.

How do you feel? *(pause)*

Look up at the sky – you can see the birds flying – imagine them flying through the wind – flying wherever they want to go – imagine you are that bird – flying.

How do you feel? *(pause)*

Along the beach you can see a small person just like you.

They walk towards you – they are smiling.

They've come to be your friend.

They take your hand and you start to run along the beach.

Feel the sun on your skin – the wind in your hair.

You feel free – happy – full of sunshine. *(pause)*

Your friend is showing you how to play a game with the seashells – join in.

Spend a few moments playing – feeling safe and happy.

At this point let them listen to the music and just continue to imagine for about 10–20 breaths.

Now it's time to leave your friend but you can come again soon.

Say 'thank you' to your friend – you are glad they are your friend.

You can play with them whenever you choose.

Wave goodbye as you walk back up the beach.

You see the door again – it is a magical door.

As you open the door you step back inside this room.

Close the door behind you.

Remember how happy and safe you were feeling.

Remember your body – tap your toes on the floor, tap your fingers.

Breathe out and open your eyes.

Using a mantra or affirmation

The word 'mantra' is defined as a sound or word repeated in meditation to aid concentration. You may encourage your children to use a word or phrase to practise meditation – using a word like 'Om' or something more generic like 'peace' or a phrase like 'I am happy'. Encourage your children to say it as they breathe out (they can silently breathe it in too). Or you can ask them to sing the word or phrase. For children under five this may be an easier and more enjoyable way for them to practise this technique.

8. Writing and Developing Your Script

My four-year-old was having a terrible time after me and his dad broke up; his behaviour was bad, he wasn't eating or sleeping and he kept wetting his bed. My mum suggested meditating with him, so I did and we haven't looked back! Within a week he was his happy self and able to tell me about his feelings. We do it every day. There's so much good in it!

Parent

So now you have the room set up, you have a better understanding of what activities meditation can involve and you realise the benefits for your child to learn and practise it. The next part is where you actually have to deliver a meditation that your child can follow and enjoy. This chapter will give you an idea, and some confidence, of how to develop your own meditations and deliver them effectively. Developing your own meditations for children will be a better experience for you both than simply using other people's scripts.

When I'm teaching the course, Calm Kids – How to Teach Children Meditation, students naturally want to use a script as it feels 'safer'. With a script, they know exactly where they are going and what they and their child will be doing. I know how anxious it can be to move away from the theory and start the practice, so I believe that learning to write a script is an essential first step.

Developing a meditation script

You now know how to start and finish a meditation (see Chapter 6). Now I'm going to show you how to develop the middle part or 'essence' of your meditation with a script that takes your child on a guided inner journey. Please note that the middle section can be whatever you choose it to be (see Chapter 7 for examples of types of meditations). When writing a meditation script, there are key steps and stages:

Stage One

1. Setting the intention for the meditation – how do you wish your child to feel during and after the meditation?
2. Choose an object and/or setting.
3. (You) relax and let go.
4. Use the senses to explore this idea in your imagination.
5. Use the self-awareness technique to help you pay attention to where the words/ideas/images come from.
6. Write it down word for word as you would wish to say it (this is very important).

Let's explore each of these steps:

1. Setting the intention

Do you wish your children to feel calm and happy? Are you trying to help them focus and concentrate? Or are you hoping that they can process some feeling or worry and let it go? Although you can't (and should not) control children in their meditation, you can set an intention about what you hope they will gain from practising. Maybe they will experience this but if they don't, just accept the result of their experience anyway. You could also ask your children how they would wish to feel during and after the meditation, thus helping them set their own personal intention too.

2. Choose an object/setting

Are you planning to guide them to a beach or a garden or a meadow or a play park? Will there be other people there? Will you focus on specific objects in that setting, such as the waves, shells, trees, flowers, swings? Or are you helping them to explore an object in their imagination and with their senses like a stone or piece of fruit? Don't go into too much detail at this stage, but a few initial ideas will help you to start imagining the setting/object. Soon you will develop a script to describe this subject and how the child interacts with it during meditation.

3. (You) RELAX AND LET GO

This is an opportunity for you to relax and feel grounded. Keep your connection with the ground (through your feet or your spine) and notice your breath to help you relax. Just set the intention that with every out-breath you let go of any tension or control of writing the script – and accept that with every in-breath there is a feeling of peace in your body. This helps you to let go and get the creative juices flowing!

Top tip: if you are struggling to get started, take a moment to relax, focus on your breath, move your attention towards the object or setting, and imagine breathing the meditation idea into your brow (for a few breaths) and notice what you see, then slide it down into your chest (the heart centre). Notice the images and feelings that start to appear.

4. USING THE SENSES

Remember that to help your children imagine their guided journey, it's helpful to draw their awareness to their different senses. Most children tend to 'see' when they use their imagination, e.g. seeing the garden or the flowers, but you can use the sense of sight more creatively than this (the number of petals in a flower, colours etc). You could bring in the sense of smell (the scent of flowers or grass), or touch (feeling the soft grass), or sound (birds tweeting).

Sometimes the question you ask can be a closed one, such as, 'Is the sea calm?' Or it might be an open ended question: 'What colour is the sea?' Use a combination of both styles of questions to help your children to explore their senses in this guided imaginary journey.

Top tip: leading your children through a meditation is a blend of describing the setting/object and asking them questions. Be aware of this but do not over-think it – just trust your intuition.

Some of these senses will be more appropriate than others to bring into a meditation. Go with what feels right. Concentrate on each sense and use it to help develop the script based around the meditation subject.

Sight – you take in a lot of information through your sense of sight but in meditation you are asking children to use their 'inner eye', more commonly known as their imagination. To help your children use this sense, you may ask them to notice:

- The size of the object (small or large)
- The shape (round, square, the shape of the petals on a flower)
- The colour
- The texture (rough or smooth)
- Any patterns/shapes
- The number of petals, leaves, flowers

Touch – some children can be more comfortable with 'feeling' rather than 'seeing' an object, so it's important to bring in different options using different senses – especially if working with a group of children. You could ask children to notice:

- The weight of the object they might be holding (light or heavy)
- If an object feels rough or smooth
- If an object feels cool or warm
- If an object has a pattern that you can feel
- Where it touches them on, or how it fits into their hands

Sound – for some objects/settings this will make more sense than with others. For example, you would not necessarily notice the sound of an apple unless you imagine biting into it. Use this sense in the following way:

- Notice if the sound is soft or loud
- Notice and follow where the sound flows to in the room
- Notice where you can feel the sound in your body (e.g. if you are using a bell or singing bowl)
- Notice a sound and count it (e.g. clock ticking)
- Notice sounds and count them one by one
- Notice a sound and 'name it'
- See the sound – either the waves of sound, their colour or what is actually creating this sound

Smell – a very primitive sense and not always one that children can imagine very easily, but again it depends on the child, so you could include this at some point and see if they can imagine or 'create' this sense of the object within the meditation setting.

Depending on the object/setting, notice if the smells are sweet, fresh, smoky, light, heavy – use any adjectives that seem appropriate.

Taste – this is only appropriate to certain objects and activities, but you could imagine tasting an apple and noticing:

- If it is sweet or sour
- Where they feel the sensation in their mouths
- The sound they make as they eat it
- The temperature (e.g. of an apple that might feel very cool and refreshing)

5. USING SELF-AWARENESS

When I refer to self-awareness I mean paying attention to your body, mind and feelings in any given moment. It is very similar to the 'on the spot' or the 'being in the moment' meditations (see p.53). It is a fantastic skill to develop, especially when teaching meditation, as it helps you to relax and enjoy it as much as your children do; you learn how to trust your own intuition to choose the best words and images to use, and it helps you to unlock ideas for your meditation. When I'm teaching students how to write their first meditation script, I usually give them an object and setting – a flower in a garden, or a shell on a beach, or a tree in a meadow. I ask them to practise self-awareness, then write down their meditation word for word.

You may think that you're already self-aware but try this little exercise to see if this is true. When you first try this, do so with your eyes closed and someone reading it out to you.

SELF-AWARENESS EXERCISE – EYES CLOSED

Close your eyes. Between each sentence pause for a few seconds or 2 breaths.

Notice your breath at the tip of your nose.

Notice the journey of the in-breath and the out-breath. Do this for several breaths.

Then with one of your out-breaths, take your attention to your body.

How does it feel?

How is your posture?

Try not to judge or change your body, just notice how it is sitting.

Does one side of your body feel different or tight compared to the other?

Is one part of your body more tense than the other? Legs? Arms and hands? Face? Shoulders? Pay gentle attention to that part of you with a sense of curiosity as if you are just realising or rediscovering your body.

Take your breath into the areas that are tense and just think about the word 'relax' as you breathe out.

Keeping doing this and watch what happens.

So, how did you feel? Were you surprised at how your body felt? Were there areas of tension or did you notice that you felt really tired or energised? This is what I call self-awareness, where we notice how the body feels. Generally speaking, unless the body is in pain, you probably don't notice how it feels. Yet you could benefit greatly from listening to and relaxing the body frequently. If you practise this with your eyes closed, with someone reading it out to you, then it's generally easier to do. It's more difficult (at first) to focus with our eyes open as we are looking outside of ourselves and paying little attention to what's going on inside.

SELF-AWARENESS EXERCISE – EYES OPEN

Have someone read this out to you. It helps if you look at the floor in front of you, relax your gaze, feet on the ground, seated in a chair. Pause after each sentence for 1–2 breaths.

Just let your gaze be soft and gentle – no hard staring.

It can help to take in your peripheral vision (looking out of the sides of your eyes) to help soften your gaze and relax.

As you do this take your attention to your breath – notice the in- and out-breath.

Then follow your breath into your body just as you did before but this time with your eyes gently open.

You might find you are distracted quite easily by what you see around you or any movement. Each time this happens, just guide your awareness into the breath, then into the body whilst keeping your gaze soft (using your peripheral vision).

Explore your body bit by bit (start at the head or feet) and just notice and be aware.

This exercise is about teaching you how to be aware whilst your eyes are open. With practice you can quickly shift your awareness into your body and notice any tension, then encourage these tense parts to relax with the breath.

If you found yourself easily distracted, don't worry. This is normal when you try this at the beginning. It takes a little bit of practice and is a great technique to learn for a number of reasons:

- It will help you learn how to relax and focus anywhere and with anyone. So you could be waiting on a bus or at a traffic light or in a meeting or the supermarket queue. Wherever you are, the point is that you soften your gaze and take your attention inside. You are aware of what is outside but you let it go.
- As a beginner in teaching meditation, it will help you to develop meditation ideas and scripts.
- It will also help you relax when you're teaching children meditation. Children respond very quickly to our anxious energy so they will feel more relaxed if you are.
- It helps you to follow your intuition and develop your inner script so that your energy goes towards the children rather than into a written script.

- Finally it helps you watch your children to see how they are meditating. Your children might be restless or disturbing others (if they're in a group), and they can easily do this if your eyes are closed. They will pay more attention and settle down if your eyes are open.

Top tip: if you start to panic about leading the meditation, just bring your awareness back to your breath to relax for a few breaths before continuing. Think of your breath as your anchor helping you to focus on the moment. You could also take your breath to your solar plexus or your feet/base of spine. The solar plexus links to the energy centre of fear so by breathing into it you relax and let go of any fears you have about leading the meditation. The feet/base of spine link to the root chakra and by taking your breath to these areas you will feel more grounded, centred and calm (see Chapter 5).

6. Write it down – word for word

So you have been practising your self-awareness and hopefully you feel the words and images flowing! Writing your meditation down word for word is a really important step for the first couple of scripts that you write, as it helps you learn how to work and feel more confident with your imagination. First of all it helps you to notice the words as they come out (even if they seem to flow faster than you can write – still write it down word for word) and it helps with Stage Two of script writing – creating meditation triggers.

To use your imagination, you use the right side of your brain (the left side is for logical, linear thought). It can take some practice if you are a logical, practical person, but persevere and it will start to develop. Perhaps after writing you re-read the script and started changing things after analysing it. This is the logical mind pulling it to pieces (which is quite normal) but for now, ignore the logical mind as we want to work with the imagination.

Developing your awareness of the imagination is important as it shows you where the words and feelings come from and helps you to trust your intuitive, creative mind. As you do this focus on your breath and try to 'feel' as well as 'see' the words and images as they appear.

This will help you further on when you're teaching meditation from what I call your 'inner script'. Ideally you would choose a different meditation idea each time you practise this exercise so you can get the experience of creating and following your imagination and intuitive mind as you write up a new 'story' (rather than simply just using your memory).

At this stage you should have several meditation scripts, and you could simply use the script to guide your child through a meditation, however physically reading out that script word for word or using other people's scripts does not give either of you the best experience. When you use a meditation script:

- You may speak too quickly and not leave enough time for your child to respond to what you are saying.
- It can sound 'false' or the meditation has an unnatural rhythm or is too fast.
- You can't participate or observe your child as your eyes are on the script.
- Your energy goes into the script (or at the very least is split between the script and your child) so you have less connection with your child.

All my experience has shown me that when I don't use a written script but work from what I call my 'inner script', people in my classes feel connected and involved, as if the pace, tone and rhythm of the meditation matches their needs. In time you will learn to develop your inner script. But before you reach that stage you need to develop some meditation triggers.

Stage Two – creating meditation triggers

Creating triggers helps you to overcome your anxiety about *not* using a script. To do this, review your written script and try to reduce it to subheadings that represent steps in the meditation. These steps become your triggers to help you remember the flow of the meditation. Don't make these long sentences – a maximum of three words for each trigger in the meditation to help you remember what the step is. For example, if part of your meditation read, 'There is a gravel path leading into a forest and you can feel the air become cooler as you move into the shade', I might choose the following trigger words:

Path
Forest
Shade

So you can see how these words would create a picture that you would start to describe using the senses. If you feel you can trust your intuition, you could simply have the word 'forest' to help you know where to guide your child.

Once you have written down these key steps for the full script, you can start to use them to practise leading a meditation. Use the self-awareness technique whilst imagining the trigger words to help you tap into your imagination. Remember, it's not about producing the most beautiful, stunning script. At this stage, it's about practising and trusting yourself whilst being self-aware.

Sit quietly and read just one trigger on the script. Imagine breathing the trigger word into your brow and imagine sliding it down into your chest for a few breaths. Take your attention into self-awareness (see p.72) and notice what words, images or feelings you sense when you consider that trigger. Now say them out loud as if you were describing this to your child. This is you starting to develop your 'inner script'; you are using the same process you used to write down a script, except you're missing out the 'writing' part. As you notice each trigger word, try to stay in self-awareness – just follow your breath into your body as this will help you stay relaxed.

Top tip: if you get anxious or your mind goes 'blank' it's because you've slipped out of your imagination (right side of brain) into your logical thought (left side of brain). Simply stop, take your attention to your breath, follow your breath, and with each out-breath relax your body. Do this for as many breaths as it takes and then go back to the trigger in a relaxed state and see what comes up from your imagination for you to describe.

It is really important for you to practise self-awareness as you guide your child in meditation. This is relevant whether you have been meditating for a long time or you're a complete beginner. It will also help you to enjoy the experience so that it doesn't feel forced. In fact you will notice, the more you practise, that you find it easier to trust your intuitive, creative mind and let go of over-thinking. The 'process' of teaching becomes like a secondary meditation for you as if you were experiencing it with your child.

Stage Three – developing your inner script

Once you have your meditation triggers in place and have practised a few times with these, you are now ready to try without any triggers or script! This is what I call developing your 'inner script'. There are many benefits for you and your children in leading a meditation this way. You will use the words, images and ideas that are suited to their needs – physically, mentally, emotionally and energetically. For you, the benefit is learning to trust in the moment whilst you are actively doing something. When you learn to do this, it means you can do it again and again, any time, any place.

You already know the stages in your mind so try to feel them instead by taking them into the chest, the area of your heart centre and *feeling* them. Breathe into your chest and when you feel ready just describe what you feel or see in your imagination. Pause when you need to, to give yourself time to be self-aware and keep yourself calm. Just keep taking yourself through the 'inner script' step by step and try to go with the flow.

What you find as you work with your inner script is that you start with an idea and a 'plan' but when you actually come to guide your child through meditation your plan can change. This can happen because you feel the words, so you say what feels right rather than simply thinking the words with your feelings switched off. It's not a logical decision to change but a feeling that feeds you the words that are totally appropriate to the children you are working with as your energy connects with theirs. When you work in this intuitive way, it feels like you are in a pool and if there is a ripple or wave, you can feel it. When you notice it, you intuitively respond with the most suitable words to smooth out the ripples. For children who are led through a meditation this way, the meditation is *always* more peaceful, calm and relevant to their needs.

The more you practise, the more you let go. The more you let go, the more you trust the creative, intuitive process that helps you to create the inner meditation script. The more you trust, the more naturally it will flow and the more you will connect and sense and feel your children around you. The more you do this, the less and less you will need the triggers and before you know it you will be heading into your meditation practice with natural curiosity – just waiting to see what turns up!

If you're struggling...

If you feel overwhelmed at first because you are new to meditation, and you don't think you could work with your inner script, you can take part in the meditation with your child so you can learn together. You could do this by recording your scripts or those I have suggested throughout the book. Alternatively you could ask another adult to use a written script and lead the meditation so you can join in.

However, ideally you should try the steps I have outlined above. In my Calm Kids – Teach Children Meditation programme, I have witnessed complete beginners or those with little confidence follow the steps above. It has been amazing and an honour to watch how their ability to trust and work with their 'inner script' unfolds in such a short space of time.

As time moves on...

You will hopefully find time to practise these meditation techniques with children on a regular basis – one that suits your schedule. You have the choice of using day-to-day activities, on the spot 1-minute meditations, trying the very simplest techniques (e.g. noticing the breath or sounds) or longer guided journey meditations. Using it during your children's usual routine (brushing their teeth, having a shower, brushing their hair) shows them how to be more self-sufficient, and it becomes a tool that they may actively choose to use in their time of need (exams or school anxiety etc).

Although this book is a reference and a useful starting point, let your own creativity flow. If something you try doesn't feel comfortable, then change it! The key is for you to enjoy it and to relax, and as you do your child will feel relaxed and enjoy it too.

As you help your children to practise regularly you may notice a peaceful bond of energy form between you and them. You can also start to suggest that they practise on their own as this empowers them with the choice to use meditation and mindfulness at stressful times throughout the day.

9. Top Tips for Teaching Meditation

I'm an office manager in a primary school. Staff know I practise yoga and mediation and the Year Five teacher asked me to show them what I do as part of their study on Buddhism. With incense sticks, Tibetan chimes and music we had a lovely session. They loved it! The most surprising were the ones who could be 'difficult'; they loved it and said they wanted to do it again and that it was 'cool'. A parent with a child in that class said that I had made a big impact on her daughter, and that she wanted flowers in a ring that she could sit and meditate in when her sister gets on her nerves!

School employee

This book is based on a course I run where I show adults how to help children meditate. Sometimes the adults can feel quite intimidated about leading meditations in front of another person for the first time. Perhaps you feel this way? You may feel a little stressed, as you probably want to deliver the meditation perfectly with no mistakes. If you feel this way, that's quite normal. This chapter will show you how to let go of the pressure to be perfect. Try to remember that whatever children experience both during and after the exercise is personal to them and not for you to judge as right or wrong. Ideally the more you can gently guide them through the meditation, but let go so that they find their own way, the more they will gain and learn from the experience.

Working one-to-one

When you are leading your child through a meditation, it's a good idea to gently watch and observe him. Let him know that you're there and that you will be watching over him. If he twitches, smiles, frowns or moves about initially, try not to react as if something is wrong. Just let go and observe. It's usually best to let your child know at the beginning that if he doesn't feel okay, to let you know and you will stop. Or you can reassure him during the meditation that he is safe and protected. It's reassuring for children to be reminded of this.

Working with one child can feel less intimidating than applying these methods to a group. You will also have more time and space to dedicate to the child and his development. Working one-to-one with your child means that you can sit closer together and therefore you can talk more quietly. I would suggest sitting opposite each other at the same level: so if he's on a chair, you sit on a chair; if he's on the floor, you can both sit on the floor.

You may even try some of the methods holding hands with your child. When I practised this with my three-year-old nephew he wanted to sit in my lap as I sat cross-legged on the floor.

Working with a group

Ideally your group should be very similar in age. Younger children have a shorter attention span and usually need a more tactile approach to meditation. If there is a large age gap you will have to develop the meditation for the youngest child in the room, regarding focus and ability to understand, and this could be boring for older children.

Ideally the group size for a session would be no more than twelve children, which may not always be possible in schools as class sizes are bigger. The larger the group the shorter the meditation should be, to accommodate all attention spans. I would suggest a session anywhere from 1–10 minutes, which should ideally be repeated a couple of times a day, so it becomes a positive habit. As they become more experienced you can gradually let the sessions run for longer. It can take some time for a large group to settle down, so it's best to start with shorter sessions until the group is more experienced.

With larger groups of more than twelve, the likelihood is that the meditation session will take place in a gym hall or classroom. I have taught meditation in many different situations but find that for a large group of children, it's a good idea to change the atmosphere somehow (see Chapter 4), to set the tone of what you're about to do. If it's not possible to get the children to remove their shoes, sit cross-legged or lie down, then at least change the lighting or burn oils so that they can be aware of some kind of change. For this size of group the meditation may simply involve focusing on the breath and relaxing their bodies, or using their favourite colour in the 'colour meditation', which is an excellent meditation to try with bigger groups. Here is a sample script of the colour meditation – remember to pause where indicated for 1 or 2 breaths. See also Chapter 8 for ideas on how to develop your own meditation scripts.

COLOUR MEDITATION

Eyes closed – imagine you are sitting in a big bubble.
This bubble is *your* bubble.
No one can enter this bubble unless you say so. *(pause)*
Imagine a colour – see what colour pops into your head – or what colour you feel. *(pause)*
Imagine the air in your bubble starts to change to that colour – it is a lovely colour – it makes you feel safe and happy. *(pause)*
Imagine the air in front of you turns into that colour. *(pause)*
Imagine the air at your sides turns into that colour. *(pause)*
Imagine the air behind you turns into that colour. *(pause)*
Imagine the air above you turns into that colour. *(pause)*
Imagine the air beneath you turns into that colour. *(pause)*
The colour feels safe, happy and warm.
Now your bubble is filled with this colour. *(pause)*
When you breathe in – imagine you breathe in the colour.
Imagine it flowing inside you. *(pause)*
Each time you breathe in that colour – you feel safer, lighter and happier.
Imagine you are like a balloon filling with that colour. *(pause)*

Now the colour is all around you and inside you – and you feel
safer, lighter and happier.
Notice how you feel. *(pause)*
When you breathe out – gently open your eyes – notice how you
feel.

If you're working with large numbers of children, sometimes it's helpful to organise a specific time in the schedule when children can choose to take part. This helps to keep the group to smaller numbers, and the act of children choosing to do this is a positive and significant indicator that the child actively wants to try meditation.

Scheduling

When is the best time to meditate? The best time is the one that suits you and your child, which allows you to practise regularly. There's no point in trying to set a rigid routine that you can't stick to. The value of meditation is realised through practice, so if you feel that you have no time to spare, then start off with short awareness meditations (focusing on the breath etc., see pp.43–59). Keep introducing these until you and your child feel calmer and ready to cope with a slightly longer meditation session and one you can fit into your schedule.

You might choose to try meditation before bedtime, which is a useful tool in helping children to unwind, especially if sleep is an issue. They can practise it whilst lying in their beds and this might be a good introduction for them. However, try to incorporate some activities at other times too. If children can learn to do this at any time, then they can use it throughout the day whenever they feel stressed.

When practising regular meditation, if you choose a time that suits both you and your child that you can stick to, then you are both more likely to practise. If you feel that you could find time to try 10 minutes or more, then start doing this either weekly, daily or every two to three days. If you're trying a shorter session of 1–3 minutes then you can practise this every day or every other day. Shorter sessions might be a good way to start and end the day to help bring you and your child into balance. If you both enjoy it then schedule it more frequently. There's no point in doing something for the sake of it – you have to enjoy the experience to ensure it doesn't feel like a chore. Just remember that regular practice does make a difference, so play around with the timings and ideas until you find a routine that you and your child are comfortable with.

Timing

It's important when teaching adults or children to start slowly with short meditations then allow them to gradually become longer. In Chapter 10, I give suggestions about attention spans and how to teach different age groups.

Body posture

Body posture is important in meditation. Whether they're lying down, sitting cross-legged or in a chair, it's important that they have a connection with the ground. If they're sitting on a chair and the soles of their feet are not flat on the floor, they need a cushion or blanket under them so that they are touching. I discuss this in more detail in the section about energy centres in the body and grounding to help relaxation and focus (see p.38).

If you're working with older children (age 7+) you ideally want them to practise seated rather than lying down to prevent them from falling asleep.

Shoes on or off?

When anyone learns meditation with me, I ask them to remove their shoes. This signals to the body and the brain that we're going to do something different and eventually it becomes associated with relaxation and meditation. The importance of touch is useful and more effective without shoes and it assists with grounding our energy. Let children wear socks if their feet are cold.

Eyes open or closed?

I would always advise children to close their eyes when they meditate and relax. This is mainly to switch off the masses of information that they take in through their sense of sight – constantly feeding their brains about the world around them. It helps to switch off that stimulus so we can access the quieter place inside.

There can be times when children find it difficult to close their eyes so I would avoid being dictatorial. Try to be sensitive and find other ways. I've found that if children have had traumatic experiences or are simply scared of the dark, they will not shut their eyes; the issue lies with a lack of trust and not feeling safe. If you find that this is the case, ask them to half close their eyes and then look at the floor just in front of their feet or body. Ask them to soften their gaze, let their eyes relax and all their muscles relax. You can ask them to see out of the 'side' of their eyes rather than looking directly ahead. This uses the peripheral vision, which helps aid relaxation.

You might find that they naturally close their eyes either further on in the meditation or in subsequent sessions and you can take this as a sign that they are starting to trust and feel safe. Let them find their own way. If they are lying on their back, they can look at a point on the ceiling but ask them to soften their gaze, looking out the side of their eyes too. You may also find that children are so curious that they close their eyes initially but then open them to have a peek. Don't let that distract you. Keep speaking to them but gesture gently for them to close their eyes. It may be that they just need a moment of reassurance to help them know where they are and where you are.

Imagination

Adults can be much harder to teach than children when it comes to using their imagination! As adults we are always 'thinking' but usually with the left side of our brains, thus analysing, judging and worrying! With children, they usually have a strong link with the right side of their brains, which link to the creative and imaginative side. The younger they are the more active this is. This can make it easier to work with children than adults using guided imagery and their imagination. Please note that some children struggle with their imagination or are older and more 'logically' minded, so other methods may be more suitable – perhaps beginning with more tactile meditation methods.

This is an example of a logical mind. If I ask you (or a logically-minded child) to think of a door and to walk through it, you may:

- Think of a door you already know of (e.g. your front door) rather than an imaginary one, and then the logical mind might take you into your house rather than following the journey of the meditation I'm trying to guide you through.
- Think of an imaginary door but then start to question the existence of this door.
- Become distracted by thoughts of the day and forget to imagine the door.

If I ask young or creative-minded children to think of a door and walk through it, they can usually imagine the door (touching, seeing, feeling) quite easily. Children are much more willing to 'play' and be imaginative so we can use colour, words, imagery, objects and more to be creative. If you say 'There is a white horse' or 'You are in a garden' then, generally speaking, they can see or feel it in their imagination. This makes teaching children meditation a lot of fun as it gives you the opportunity to tap into your creative side too! To help with a logically-minded child I would suggest you frequently say 'Be curious and let your imagination go' to encourage them to let go of their 'hold' on logic.

Please note that when working with the imagination and especially with very young children (age 6 or younger) you have to ensure they know the difference between what is 'real' and what is imagined. Children are still developing and they don't always know the difference between their imagination and reality. For example, if you guide them on a visualisation about flying, then you may wish to give them some safe imagery like a magic carpet to fly on or get them to imagine climbing into an aeroplane, rather than simply asking them to believe they can fly. This is something you should make clear to them after sessions too; that the place they 'visit' on their journey is an imaginary place – their imagination is the place for flying.

Language skills

When working with children, use a level of language that they understand for the majority of the meditation. Common sense tells us that it's not helpful to lead a child through meditation as we would an adult, using complicated or 'big words'. However one of my students (a teacher) advised that the occasional 'big word' is okay, as this is how children learn and develop.

As you guide them, if you mention a particular flower, for example a lily, they may not know what the flower looks like. In this instance, you might start to describe the colour, shape of the petals, size of the stem etc. Even if they do know this type of flower, still ask them to use their senses of smell, sight and touch to bring it alive in their imagination.

As a parent or teacher you will already be familiar with your children's level of understanding, so please tailor your guided meditations accordingly. Here are some examples of how you can adapt language.

Adult	Child
'Acknowledge your thoughts and let them go.'	'For this moment, blow your thoughts away...'
'Take your attention to your breath.'	'Feel your breath – in through your nose and out through your mouth.'
'Imagine a path escalating up a mountain.'	'Look at the ground and you see a path. You follow the path as it moves around a mountain. Step by step you start to follow the path up and around the mountain.'

Pace

The most common error that people make when they're trying to guide a child through a meditation is that they speak too quickly. This is usually down to nerves and a fear of silence, which we are accustomed to filling with chatter. When you are guiding children through their meditation, don't rush. Give them time to acknowledge what you've said, especially if you're asking them a question such as, 'How do you feel at this moment?' When you do this, take one or two long deep breaths to help you pause, which will calm you and help you to maintain a suitable pace. When you ask them how they're feeling in that moment, this gives them the opportunity to notice a feeling they would like to release or to acknowledge how happy they feel. Using gentle commands and questions such as 'Keep listening to my voice' or 'How does your body feel?' can help children to stay in the moment, know where they are, and notice how it feels to be in this peaceful place. Don't be afraid of silence!

Coping with noise

Unless we live on the moon, noticing noise and sound during meditation is usually unavoidable so we must learn to accept it. However adults are usually more bothered by noise than children.

I've witnessed this in schools where I've been leading sessions with children and there are voices over loudspeakers and bells ringing, yet the children have just continued with their meditation as if nothing has happened – it's amazing! This has led me to realise that children can cope with noise so the environment doesn't need to be completely quiet for them to meditate. If anything, a little bit of noise can be comforting – reminding them that the real world is still there. If you live next to a busy road or live in a busy household then the likelihood is that they've already become accustomed to this.

What is important during this time is to let yourself relax too and not be distracted. If you're tense then children will notice this (even with their eyes closed) through the tone and pace of your voice. So try to relax your own body as you ask them to relax theirs, have your feet on the ground so your energy is focused and grounded, and relax your breathing too.

If you've taken the opportunity to sit down to try these exercises with your children then make sure you're not disturbed. Whilst children can cope with noise, if there's a sudden, loud noise outside or someone bursts into the room where you're meditating, it is anything but relaxing. So make sure others in the house know they are not to disturb – hang a sign on the door and switch off phones.

If you think children are struggling with noise, you can simply add in statements such as 'Notice the sounds but let them go' and then guide them back to the meditation.

Developing your meditation practice with children

Here is a quick reminder to help you develop your meditation practice with children:

- Watch your speed – this is where nerves take hold and you speak too quickly. Your children may not have heard you correctly, so remember to repeat the phrase a couple of times. Or they might need time to adjust and feel/sense/see what you are asking them to experience.
- Remember to breathe – it helps you to relax.
- Silence is okay – allow there to be moments of silence.
- Stay grounded – feeling centred and trusting that the right words will come out. Keep your feet or base of spine touching the floor.
- You will make mistakes – do not panic. If you get distracted and you make a mistake – trust me – it's unlikely your child will notice.
- Accept noise – if there's noise outside, just ignore it – that's life!
- If you feel silly or embarrassed – accept it and think about the amazing skill you are teaching yourself and your children.
- Your child may move around – this can be normal for some children so use your words to guide them to rest or keep their feet on ground.
- If you panic it will be because you are ungrounded and have forgotten your breath – so ensure you have contact with the ground and focus on your breath.
- The energy of the group is like the chicken and egg scenario. When they are calm, you are calm – when you are calm, they are calm. Keep your tone soft and relaxed and take the pace slowly and gently.

Your role in teaching meditation

I have noticed differences between teaching children and adults meditation. It would be misleading for me to say that children find it easier than adults to meditate or vice versa. Both groups have their own challenges and I have learned from experience that there is no perfect formula. We are human beings and therefore quite unique in our mental and emotional experiences, regardless of age. Perhaps you have lots of experience practising meditation but have never tried teaching it before. Or perhaps you are completely new to meditation. One of the beautiful aspects of teaching meditation is that the process teaches you too. If you're experienced you learn how to practise a living, breathing meditation, guiding your children using words (and no script) that feel right. For the inexperienced you learn to let go and practise self-awareness as you teach (great skills for your own personal well-being). For both the experienced and inexperienced it's a step towards learning to trust: trust in yourself, trust in life, and trust in your heart. It's a profound experience and a wonderful step for you and your child.

Let go, observe and accept

A leader is best when people barely know he exists, when his work is done, his aim fulfilled, they will say: we did it ourselves.

Lao Tzu

Teaching children how to meditate is not a method for a parent or teacher to control children. Parenting and teaching children is a continual learning process and a very challenging, yet rewarding, experience. Meditation is a *very personal* choice. You can gently guide children but you can't force them to meditate as this totally defeats the essence of what meditation is – letting go and developing awareness of their own intuitive voice.

The likelihood is that they will listen to you and trust you, so they will want to do what you ask them to. At the very least they may wish to copy you if you meditate with them.

If you attempt to meditate with them and they don't want to, ask them why. Perhaps you can change the meditation to suit their needs. If they strongly resist taking part then let it go, as it's just not the right time or the right method for them and consider the other options of moving meditations such as Tai Chi or Yoga. Perhaps you can get them involved in the process of choosing what aspect of meditation they would like to try. Instead of 'Would you like to practise meditation?' ask if they would they like to try a breathing or colour activity (keep the choices to two so it's simple). By giving them a choice they will usually feel more empowered when they choose what's right for them. Adults think they know best (usually we do) but in the case of meditation it's such a personal journey that we must respect each individual (children, too) to choose for themselves. Listen to your children and encourage them to practise the methods they enjoy. This is common sense as they will be more likely to practise meditation in their own time and space if they enjoy it!

As an adult trying to teach your child meditation it's useful to start by letting go of any expectations you have of 'how' your child should behave in a meditation. There is no 'how' but simply an unconditional approach to trying different techniques and observing the results. Try to release your expectations and maintain a childlike curiosity about what the meditation will be for your children. Whilst you are teaching your children meditation, realise that they are teaching you how to let go and be calm 'in the moment' with them.

When we choose to practise meditation techniques with our children, we do this as we ultimately wish to bring more peace into their lives (and ours). All these benefits make meditation a very attractive antidote to the stress of life and it gives them the life-long skill of how to tap into feelings of peace, happiness and self-esteem. However it's important to realise that while this is an intention you can set for your children it's not the end goal. When you set an intention, you're identifying how you hope your children will feel and think, but it's important to let go of the outcome and accept whatever they experience, which reflects how their energy is at this moment in time.

When using meditation techniques with children think of it as a journey where instead of paying attention to the destination (end goal), we choose to go in this direction (intention) with our children and then we pay attention to each step and its experiences (meditation). You can set your intention but it's important to have no expectations of how your children should be or respond during the meditation. If they giggle or yawn or wriggle or feel sad, then this is okay. Let them experience this and let go.

Children may be quite physically restless during meditation and you can gently encourage them to stay still, but even if they remain restless, be aware that this is *their* experience. I have observed that if children feel they're being controlled, they sense it and kick back against it. Consider how you would feel if someone was gently guiding you through a meditation compared to controlling you; the experience would be totally different. When I first started teaching children's classes I was amazed at how some children (aged 5–6) tossed and turned – leaving me to think they were not benefiting from the experience. Yet afterwards the children would give me the most interesting feedback on what they felt or saw. I realised that I had to overcome my own prejudices of how people should behave during meditation and simply let them be. This particular group of children came from very challenging backgrounds so perhaps the restlessness reflected how agitated their energy was in daily life.

Even if you use the same meditation with them each time, it's likely that they'll have a different experience each time. None of us think the same thoughts or feel the same way each day or each moment in a day. We are constantly learning, changing and developing. Thus when we try the same meditation we can have different thoughts, emotions or physical responses as the meditation practice helps us come back into balance. Sometimes your child's meditation will feel easy and other times it may feel challenging. Meditation can help release physical and emotional tension, which can present itself as pain, or awareness of negative or busy thoughts. This is not a 'wasted' meditation, but offers children an opportunity to process and release these feelings so that they can let go and eventually feel more peaceful.

Let go
Observe
Accept

These three fundamental steps help you and your children to share moments of meditation in a way that deepens their experience and your sense of inner peace and calm. As you start to expand your awareness of what meditation can be, then you can start to let go and enjoy meditation and mindful activities with your children, with no expectations but simply being in the moment.

Take the first step in faith. You don't have to see the whole staircase, just take the first step.

Martin Luther King Jr

10. Working with Different Age Groups

I taught my children meditation when they were five years old. They are all grown up now and practise daily meditation. My daughter teaches it to her music students.

Parent

When I first started teaching meditation I believed that you could only teach children over a certain age as I thought it was limited to their ability to comprehend and their attention and energy levels. I have changed my mind since then. Meditation and mindfulness activities can be made available to all ages and abilities – it's just a question of adapting them to the needs and abilities of the child.

Please note the suggested timings for each age group include any breath work, relaxation and bringing them back into the moment.

Babies

Strictly speaking it's not the baby that will be meditating but the person holding them. As the adult calms their energy while gently holding or stroking, the baby will respond to this. I expand on this in the next chapter.

Toddlers (age 2–3)

For toddlers, meditation can help with two areas – to develop focusing skills and to wind down before bedtime. The meditation is more of a focusing activity, with a tactile approach when noticing the breath (such as, holding hands in front of mouth and nose, making a sound as they breathe out), moving with the breath (lifting arms up and down), stretching and curling up with the breath, using rhymes, using colour (where you 'colour them in'), and using the sense of touch (stroking them from their heads down to their toes, which is very good for grounding their energy).

Attention span for this would be anything from 1 minute (repeated regularly) to a maximum of 5 minutes.

I was practising with my nephew before bedtime. We did some progressive muscle relaxation to help him focus and relax then a short colour meditation and a short journey to a beach (See Chapter 12 for more information).

Young children (age 4–6)

Meditations would usually be shorter and more focused, with a short time spent on tactile relaxation. They will be more interested in the 'story' of the guided meditation and the journey that you are taking them on. The meditation can help them move to a place of peace, safety and which makes them feel light and happy. Remember, they do not put up such a logical, natural resistance and their imaginations are usually quite prepared to go with the guided journey.

Usually meditations would last up to a maximum of 10–15 minutes.

One of the groups of children I worked with at a local school was aged approximately six. I noticed that they tossed and turned a lot, so I asked them to lie down with space around them to stretch out. This helped them to relax. I used the colour meditation (see p.83) to help them relax their bodies, then we went on a magic-carpet journey and I took them to a peaceful place where they were able to explore and play. Despite the tossing and turning, when I asked the children afterwards to describe their journey, each one described the most amazing places and colours they had experienced.

Older children (age 7–12)

It's tricky trying to categorise children within this broad age bracket, as what they know, learn and understand can vary immensely – some girls at age twelve can seem to be emotionally and physically advanced for their age. Guided meditations that help them to offload worries (e.g. imagining that they are dropping stones into a pond and each one represents a worry; releasing worry bags or boxes out of a plane and feeling the plane become lighter and faster) are an excellent way to help their energy feel lighter and more free. Sitting and meditating with them using Tibetan bells or singing bowls will be very effective in helping to balance their energy. Incorporating words like 'calm' (on the in-breath) and 'peace' (on the out-breath) will help them stay focused and calm, and is something they can use in their own time too.

With practice, this age group can usually stay focused for up to 20 minutes in longer meditations.

I worked with a group of children at a local school who had never meditated before. I asked them to sit cross-legged. We spent a short time on awareness and relaxation with the breath, and I asked them to hold their hands in the grounding mudra position (where the tip of the thumb and first finger of each hand touch, see p.116). I guided them on a journey (as I mentioned above) using the idea of dropping bags of worries out of a plane, which helped them feel lighter and more peaceful. At the end of the meditation, each child reported how much happier and peaceful they felt.

Teenagers and young adults (age 12+)

I introduced meditation to my own kids. It helped while studying for their exams. The attention to breath has been good practice for them.

Parent

In this day and age children seem to be more streetwise and fashion conscious than in my childhood days. Overexposure to marketing campaigns and the media have probably contributed to this. However it's important for you to acknowledge that the transition from child to adult is a tough time emotionally, physically and mentally. For this group in particular, working with awareness of the breath and how to reduce anxiety or relax the body are very important for helping to keep their thoughts, emotions and bodies in balance. The stress of exams, their sexuality, how they look, bullying and their self-esteem can cause a great deal of anxiety. If you can encourage them to use meditation that helps them to stay grounded and calm, they will feel much better within themselves as they learn how to listen and calm their energy through these challenging times.

Remember to avoid using music with this group as music is closely associated with their personal identity – nothing you play will suit their tastes.

With this age group you will find the need to help them relax their bodies and breathing more, as moving into adulthood brings in the distraction of the logical mind. They can use breathing meditations (see examples on pp.46–48) as 'on the spot' meditations to help with anxiety, and the relaxation stage (see pp.48–51) to help them sleep better whilst studying for exams.

Usually a meditation can last for up to 20–25 minutes.

I remember working with young people at a local school. They were aged fifteen and I had been asked to teach them some Indian Head Massage techniques for stress. I took one look at the amount of hair product they used and decided that this perhaps wasn't such a good idea! Also they were quite boisterous and the teacher present seemed happy to hand the reins over to me. I decided to do a colour meditation technique with them and within 5 minutes you could have heard a pin drop as the room was so silent.

11. Meditation with Babies

I taught my boys how to meditate to the sound of 'Ah' – they loved it. We did it before naps and bed, helping them sleep soundly. They are now eight and three years old, but I taught them aged six and one.

Parent

I was approached by friends whose children were younger than those I had worked with before, so I asked them to try different methods and give me their feedback.

First of all, let me be realistic. You can't teach your baby to meditate, so when I talk about meditation for babies, the methods are really to help you as a parent or carer to relax when you're with your baby. If you are grounded and relaxed then your baby will respond positively to this – your energy affects their energy.

Babies are very sensitive to their environment and energy, which is one of the reasons they will cry. Provided there is no other obvious reason, like hunger, a baby may be upset due to the energy of the person around them who may feel agitated or anxious or feel any other negative emotion.

I first noticed this with my friend's son David when we were babysitting. David was quite content as we played and spoke to him; he seemed very happy. Another friend came into the room and before we could blink he was letting out blood-curdling cries for no apparent reason. Every time she came near him he turned away and continued crying. We were confused as my friend is a really great person and fabulous with kids. When she left the room he started to calm down.

Now let me give you some context to this story. My friend had recently lost her husband to cancer and that morning had returned from church quite upset because the service had reminded her of her grief, and she had felt a mixture of feelings about it – sadness and anger. She was talking about this (and still feeling this) when she came into the room to see David – and the baby had sensed this energy and started to wail. After 30 minutes, by which time my friend had calmed down, David happily let her play and talk to him.

Please don't think that for one moment that you can avoid having difficult feelings or emotions – we are all human after all! However, if you are aware of how your energy affects your baby, then when you are with them you can try to focus on staying calm and centred. Lots of people naturally do it anyway, but it's when you're in a stressful situation that you become 'ungrounded' and the baby picks up on this. The more you focus and stay calm and aware, the more you will manage to do this when a stressful situation arises. Let me give you an example. You are meeting up with other people and you want your baby to behave. You start to feel anxious about the meeting and worry about the baby crying. You can almost guarantee that the baby will cry as they pick up on your stress!

As a parent you are under a lot of pressure with so many demands on your time and energy, so the more you can do to stay calm the better.

Top tip: the following methods are to help you stay relaxed in the first instance. If you can use your imagination easily then use the visual imagery approach. If you're more of a tactile person then 'feel' rather than 'see'. You can use both if you want to – some people are both tactile and imaginative.

BEING GROUNDED

To be centred and grounded, start off by focusing on your solar plexus (the area just under your ribs in the centre).
Imagine/feel a point of light there.
When you breathe in think 'peace' and on the out-breath think 'love'.
Imagine/feel as if you're attaching your breath to the solar plexus light.

Feel/imagine the light glowing brighter, clearer and bigger with each breath.

Continue doing this for 5–10 breaths (eyes open or closed – it's up to you).

If it helps you to focus, you can also place your hand on the area of your solar plexus when you breathe in 'peace' and breathe out 'love'.

Now breathe down to your feet and imagine/feel a point of light in the sole of each foot.

Breathe out of the points of light in your feet and then imagine/feel the breath coming from the ground into your feet.

Use the words 'peace' with the in-breath and 'love' with the out-breath.

Do this for 5–10 breaths.

If it helps you focus, just lightly tense your feet on the in-breath and relax them on the out-breath whilst using the words.

Loving breath

Now take your attention to your heart centre – in the centre of your chest. Imagine a point of light in your chest that you attach to your breath (or just notice the rise and fall of your chest with the breath) and when you feel ready, start to breathe in the word 'peace' into your chest/point of light and the word 'love' out of your chest/point of light.

Continue for 5–10 breaths.

At this point you can be holding your baby (or if they are sleeping in their cot just hold your hands above them with palms facing them or gently touch their tummy).

Imagine/feel that 'loving' out-breath is now flowing around your baby, cocooning them in your loving breath (coming from your chest).

Continue doing this with each breath as long as you wish.

You may wish to imagine the out-breath is like a soft pink or white cloud that flows out from your heart centre and surrounds your baby.

Continue doing this with each breath as long as you wish.

You may wish to close (or half close) your eyes if you're getting distracted by your baby.

Each time remember that the in-breath is peace, and the out-breath from your chest is a loving pink or white cloud that surrounds your baby.

After 20 breaths (or more – go with what feels right) you can gently notice how you feel and notice what your baby is doing. You may start to imagine that you're both surrounded in this loving cloud.

It's a good idea to practise this often as it only takes a few minutes. You might do this after each nappy change so it coincides with a regular activity. Just remember that the more you keep doing this, the more relaxed you will be and the more your baby will notice this. Plus, once you get accustomed to doing this, you will have something to try when your baby is upset – another tool in your parent box!

12. Meditation for Toddlers

My son's nursery did yoga and meditation and all the kids loved it so much they set up a permanent quiet space which all the kids use.

Parent

I was never sure about whether toddlers could really meditate but my young nephew, Ryan, who was aged three at the time, proved me wrong! Children of this age like to copy so it's a good idea for you as the adult to participate and demonstrate what you want them to do as you guide them.

Strictly speaking, the suggested activities are not meditation or mindfulness (in the purest sense) but they do help toddlers focus their attention. If you are particularly creative then add a tune to the words. Children also like rhymes. When I gave my sister-in-law the techniques to try, my nephew Ryan expected them to rhyme. So thanks to Ryan I have given you a rhyming example, but feel free to make up your own.

I have found that trying something that is grounding will help the toddler feel calmer and can be a useful tool for the bedtime routine or during the day.

STRETCH AND SOFT (PROGRESSIVE MUSCLE RELAXATION, TODDLER-STYLE)

Standing
Stand on your tiptoes. *You may have to help them balance.*

Then feet back down on the floor. *Repeat 2–3 times.*
Touch the sky. *Arms and hands up.*
And count to 4. *You count for them if they are too young.*
Swing your arms down like a monkey. *Swing arms down and from side to side – loose – several times.*
Like you just don't care. *Stand up straight.*
Then roll your head. *Rotate head in circles or side to side – several times.*
Like a noisy bear. *You can make roar noises if you want!*
Now sit on the floor. Legs out in front.
Point your toes to me.
Point your toes to you. *Repeat several times.*
Stick out your belly.
And your tongue too.
Belly soft, tongue back in.
Give yourself a big hug.
What a good boy/girl you have been!

Now lying down
Follow my finger. *Head still, just eyes moving.*
And look to your left.
Follow my finger.
And look to your right.
Up
Down
All around. *Repeat circle of eyes one way, then the other whilst they think/say the word 'calm'.*
Hands on your tummy.
And close your eyes.
Breathing in a big breath.
Breathing out with a sigh.
Breathing in another big breath.
Breathing out with a big sigh.
Feeling softer and softer.
Like clouds in the sky.
Breathing in.

> Breathing out.
> Feel soft and calm.
> Like clouds in the sky.
> Feel soft and calm.
> Feel soft and calm.

You can repeat each section a few times before moving on to the next step but the idea is to help them ground, and therefore calm, their energy. Here are some other methods for you to try at any time throughout the day:

STRETCHING

> Stand with your legs wide and then stretch your arms up and out like a starfish. *Head straight up, feet flat on the ground. Hold for a count of 4.*
> Then crouch down to become small like a tiny mouse. *Ask them to curl in as tight as they can. Hold for a count of 4.*
> *Repeat as many times as you wish, focusing on the movement as it helps to work the body (and the chakras). They may move quickly from one position to the next but after several repetitions, ask them to do it more and more slowly.*

'AHHH' AND 'MMMM' – FOCUS

> Sitting or standing, with mouth and eyes open – take a big breath in.
> Now as you breathe out make a sound like, 'Ahhhh'. *Repeat this several times and encourage them to make the 'Ah' for as long as they comfortably can.*
> With eyes and mouth closed – take a big breath in through your nose.

Now as you breathe out through your mouth – make a sound like, 'Mmmm'.

Repeat this several times and encourage them to make the 'Mmmm' as long as they comfortably can. You can ask them to notice on one of the repetitions where they feel the sound in their bodies. This works the throat chakra and helps provide focus.

Circle

Sitting or standing, and use your finger to guide them.

Eyes up, eyes down, eyes left, then right.

Eyes all around (one direction).

Then all around (the other direction).

This helps connect and balance the logical and emotional parts of the brain. You may want to say 'up to the sun' 'down to the ground' or similar phrases as you ask them to do this.

Tapping – focus and balance

Ask children to think of something that makes them happy like their favourite toy or game and to keep thinking about that as they tap.

Tap the top of the head with your fingers.

Soft at first like snow falling.

Stronger now like rain. Or *you can tap for them.*

Tap around the eyes.

Under the nose.

On your chin.

Beat your chest (like Tarzan).

Then under the arms (like a monkey).

This technique taps different energy points and is a calming method. You can add noises to the tapping if you wish. Repeat several times.

TUMMY TIME

Lying down or standing – hands on belly button.
Breathe into your hands and push them up with your tummy.
Then breathe out and say, 'Ahhh'.
Breathe into your hands and push them up with your tummy.
Then breathe out and say, 'Mmmm'.
Encourage them to push out their tummies when they breathe in (demonstrate to them) and then the tummy relaxes when they breathe out. This works the diaphragm, which helps send signals to the brain saying 'relax'. We use this method of breathing when we are sleeping.

COLOUR MEDITATION

Choose the colour red, or if they don't like it they can choose any colour.
Ask your children to imagine this colour. You can also hold up something in this colour and ask them to say the colour out loud.
Now ask them to imagine the air around is this lovely colour.
It's on this side. *Gently stroke one arm.*
It's on this side. *Gently stroke the other arm.*
It's behind you. *Gently stroke their backs and legs.*
It's in front of you. *Gently stroke their chests and legs.*
Now get them to close their eyes and ask them to imagine that they can take the colour inside their bodies through the top of their heads and down to their toes.
You may wish to pretend that you are 'colouring them in' – gently stroking down their bodies to their feet.
As you do this say words like, 'I am safe/calm/happy', and ask them to repeat them.
This can be a very calming way to get toddlers to focus. The colour represents the chakra that is balancing.

HOLDING HANDS MEDITATION

Sit in front of each other, cross-legged, and hold hands.
Try to breathe in together and breathe out together.
Ask your children to think of things they like, people they like and
  other nice things.
As they do this, imagine you are surrounding them in a pink bubble.
Stay in this way as long as you wish.
The colour pink is the colour of the heart centre – unconditional love.

THE FLOPPY SOCK

Courtesy of my nephew Ryan who inspired me to write this.
There was a little boy called Ryan
Who was getting ready for bed
But his body felt full of beans
And there were lots of thoughts in his head. *Action – tapping*
  crown of head with fingertips.
So his mummy had an idea –
A really great way to feel calm –
He reached up his hands on his in-breath. *Action – hands up to sky.*
And on his out-breath he said a big, 'Ahhh'. *Action – hands down.*
Breathing in
His body filled up with air. *Action – hands up.*
So much air that he couldn't talk.
And each time he breathed out. *Action – hands down and 'Ahhh'.*
His body went soft.
So soft like a big floppy sock! *Action – all floppy, arms down.*
Keep doing actions.
In – filling up.
Out – floppy sock.
In – filling up.
Out – floppy sock.

13. Children with Attention Deficit Hyperactivity Disorder (ADHD)

I was privileged to teach meditation to our primary school during an awareness week. The kids really took to it although some parents objected and were allowed to take their child out of class while it went on. I had to work with one very disruptive boy one-on-one. The teachers said they had never seen him keep so still – ever!

Teacher

I first became interested in teaching children meditation in 2003, when I realised that they would really benefit from learning these methods. As many people have realised through their own experiences, these simple techniques help to reduce and manage the effects of stress.

I found myself becoming interested in children who demonstrate ADHD symptoms (attention deficit hyperactivity disorder). This interest was based on my observations of adults in my beginners' meditation classes. Some adult students, although not diagnosed with ADHD, demonstrated some very similar behaviour to that of ADHD. This was always quite apparent at the beginning of the meditation course. However, by the end of the course they seemed to have reduced or eliminated these behaviours.

The ADHD traits they demonstrated in class included the student appearing to be 'ungrounded': unable to focus, their mind full of thoughts and unable to sit still without fidgeting. Sometimes the students talked about their problems with sleep or energy levels. As I observed them in the meditation class, these students appeared to 'settle' more easily with each passing week. Their energy seemed to become calmer and more balanced with each week of practice. They seemed to become more grounded and were sleeping better. They found they could focus more easily. All these changes in my adult class suggested to me that perhaps we could try these techniques with children who were diagnosed as having ADHD.

Attention deficit hyperactivity disorder is an interesting area of health, and research tends to suggest that there are many factors contributing to the condition. The following information is based on my experience as a healer and meditation tutor. It may be of use for you to try these ideas that will complement, but should never replace, any medical support your child is receiving.

A child's development from a meditative/energy perspective

The main reason I talk about the connection between meditation and energy is because it influences us whether we are young or old. Having some awareness of the energy system of the chakras is useful in understanding a child's health and development. (I describe these in full in Chapter 5). The energy centres should not be viewed in a hierarchical way; those at the bottom (root, sacral, solar plexus) are not less significant or less important than those at the top (heart, throat, brow and crown).

All the energy centres are important and work together – just as different systems within the body work together (nervous system, circulatory, muscular, skeletal etc.). We need all of them to work well in order to live healthily. Energy is meant to flow and, provided that it does, then generally speaking, we should be in good health – physically, mentally and emotionally.

I have put together reference tables below to show how some of the symptoms of ADHD compare to energy centre imbalances. Energy centres can be guided back into balance with the help of meditation and holistic approaches. I have suggested some meditation methods that might help with these symptoms. For Attention Deficit Disorder (ADD) see the 'impulsive' and 'inattention' qualities listed on pages 111 and 112.

Root centre (base of spine) and hyperactivity

I would like to share how our hyperactive kid does his meditation – stretched/flopped over his huge gym ball, balancing himself ... quietly, zen-like, as he listens to the meditation CD in the background. At some point during this session, he'll be head touching floor, toes pointing outward, off the floor. There seems to be some sort of body balancing going on. As he's not a child who will sit still, and is constantly on the go and fidgeting away ... his kinaesthetic body seems to like the bounciness of the rubber ball. And finally, the session will come to a point whereby my kid is draped flopped over his huge gym ball, like a soft toy. Quiet. Calm. Zen – out. You can see through his eyes, he is somewhere else. For like five minutes. And then he's awake, energetically bouncing off his ball and off to his toys.

Parent

The root centre connects us to the ground and the physical world. The main colour associated with it is red, and also black and brown. This energy centre governs the blood, spine, adrenal glands and nervous system. A compulsion to move links to the root centre trying to rebalance itself. Movement is a grounding activity.

Symptoms of hyperactivity*	Symptoms of root centre imbalance (being 'ungrounded')	Grounding activities
Fidgeting with hands or feet Squirming in seat Running about excessively and inappropriately	Not able to focus Obsession with possessions Domineering Aggressive Sleeplessness Can't relax Obsessive compulsive disorders	Running Walking Eating Moving meditation Grounding meditation Grounding crystals (usually red, brown or black) Stone meditation Music with a deep, steady drumbeat (see 'Resources' p.149)

*Please note that the ADHD symptoms listed are taken from www.netdoctor.co.uk.

Throat centre and impulsiveness

The throat chakra is our expression centre – where we express our will through our choices and decisions. The colour associated with it is bright blue/turquoise. It governs the throat area – throat, thyroid, nerves and the ears, which is why some children do not listen but talk too much when this centre is unbalanced. The throat centre can be over or under active. Sound can play a key role in helping this energy centre to rebalance.

Symptoms of impulsiveness	Symptoms of throat centre imbalance	Balancing activities
Blurting out answers before the question is complete Unable to wait for his/her turn Interrupting or intruding on others	Arrogance Talks too much Addiction Timid Secretive	Colour meditation Working with crystals (usually sky blue or clear) Meditations where children say an affirmation out loud (if they are too timid, they can imagine saying it out loud and through time they may start to physically say the affirmation). Singing Toning/chanting

Root and throat centres and inattention

I have a niece who has attention problems. Since she was a small child, I have tried to meditate with her. We did the candle meditation where we stared at the candle flame for a few moments and then closed our eyes and tried to see the flame in our third eye. It worked well.

Auntie

As I have mentioned, the root centre helps us to feel grounded and safe, and the throat chakra links to how we communicate and listen.

In energy terms, inattention occurs when there is too much energy in the upper chakras (brow, throat) and not enough in the root chakra. The energy is unevenly distributed. When the energy is grounded into the root chakra, we are able to focus and complete projects.

When there is too much energy in the throat chakra it's as if it is pouring out (words) and blocking the ability to listen.

If someone is ungrounded, there is often too much energy in the brow chakra – lots of thoughts and ideas – and sometimes children can seem like they're in a world of their own. Meditation and mindfulness help to balance the brow chakra.

Symptoms of inattention	Symptoms of root/throat/brow centre imbalance	Balancing activities
Poor attention to detail. Makes careless mistakes in schoolwork, work or other activities Has difficulty in sustaining attention Does not appear to listen when spoken to Does not follow instructions Does not finish tasks Has difficulty organising tasks and activities Avoids or dislikes tasks that require sustained mental effort	Difficulty completing projects/sentences Easily distracted and jumps from one area to the next ('butterfly mind') Difficulty in listening to others – constantly talking/ignoring instructions Carrying on as if in their own world	See root and throat chakra suggestions above Brow chakra – being in the moment meditation with the breath or senses helps to balance the thinking logical mind with the creative mind. Also practising the suggestions for the root chakra helps energy to be more evenly distributed around the body.

If we compare the symptoms of hyperactivity and inattention with the behaviour of someone who has an imbalance in the root, throat and crown energy centres, we can see some similarities. During a conversation with someone whose child was diagnosed with ADHD, I mentioned that she might like to try using crystals. I suggested that her son should choose the crystals he wanted to keep in his pocket rather than his mum logically choosing 'grounding' crystals based on what she had read. When she told me about the ones he liked, they turned out to be grounding crystals anyway. So his own energy was choosing what he needed to come back into balance. For information, the crystals he was drawn to were obsidian (black) and jasper (red). If you decide that a crystal might aid your children's meditation or be a calming tool, encourage them to choose their own crystals rather than choosing for them (you can always research the meaning of the crystals afterwards).

If you have children with ADD or ADHD you may find meditation a bit challenging at first. It depends on their age, but meditations should be shorter than usual for their age group (see Chapter 10). Gentle perseverance is required and in this chapter I have listed some suggestions to help you make the most of the meditation experience, or you could purchase my meditation CD for children with ADHD (see 'Resources', p.148).

As I was writing this book, I was conducting some research with children who had been diagnosed with ADHD and also those on the autistic spectrum. Below I have written up case studies of working with two very different children and what the experiences taught me about working with children who have ADHD.

Case study with Alex

Alex was diagnosed with ADHD at age of twelve but had been displaying these symptoms for a couple of years. On a visit to the doctor with his mum, out of the blue he asked if he could be put on medication as he knew something was wrong and wanted help. He could not focus, concentrate, sit still etc. This came as a surprise to his mum but the doctor obliged, giving him medication.

I visited the family at their home at the request of the mother, who had been signposted to me through the head teacher of her son's school. On meeting Alex, I realised that even though he was on medication, he found it really difficult to sit still and moved around and fidgeted in his chair. I also felt that he was unsure about taking part and a little shy. I guessed he was there because his mum thought it was a good idea. This is normally the case, when parents feel they are at their wits end and are looking for anything to help them cope with the situation they find themselves in. I explained that we would do a short relaxation session with a bit of guided imagery to help offload worries. Alex was leaving primary school and moving into his high school so was growing anxious about the future.

Both Alex and his mum sat on the sofa with their feet touching the ground. Although he was unsure of participating, I suggested he watched his mum and join in if he wanted to. I felt that the mother really wanted to encourage her son to do this too (remember what I said about *not* trying to *make* someone meditate), but eventually she agreed to try on her own at first.

Meditation

I took Mum through some simple relaxation techniques to help her relax her body. We used the grounding hand mudra (see p.116) to help with this. Alex continued to fidget but was watching his mum as she started to relax. About halfway through the relaxation, Alex decided to join in. I noticed that as he sat with his eyes closed his energy and body language became calmer. We then progressed onto the colour breathing meditation (see p.83). During the meditation, I mentioned a 'door' that they could walk through. We used the guided imagery of going up in an aeroplane to offload baggage to make the aircraft lighter. After the imaginary journey I guided them back to their breath and eventually instructed them to open their eyes. Alex had managed to sit still for 10 minutes, quietly focusing on the meditation as I had guided him and his mum. For someone with ADHD, who had not been willing to participate originally, this was a remarkable achievement.

Feedback

When we discussed the experience afterwards, Alex explained that he had been able to visualise the images and he felt a bit better and calmer. However he had not entered a door (which I had mentioned) but had imagined a red triangle. The significance of this is important, as red is one of the most grounding colours you can use in meditation and anyone with ADHD is, from an energy perspective, not as grounded as they could be. The triangle is very symbolic in meditation terms as it has a strong base (foundation/root) reaching up to a point. The base represents an example of grounding. The fact that Alex himself saw or chose this suggests that his own inner sense of balance was trying to come through in the meditation.

Observations

The above example shows how important it is to respect children when teaching them meditation. If we had tried to force Alex to join in, the likelihood is that he would have resisted trying at all. Giving him some space to make his own decision was the best choice. When he did join in, he followed his own awareness – he did not just 'see' a door because I mentioned it but went with his own intuition. Adults may have had a logical 'fight' to see a door rather than just accept what they imagined, whereas Alex just accepted what he saw and the shape and colour of the door were completely appropriate for him. For me, the significant response was his ability to sit still after joining in the meditation – a clear, physical sign that something had changed (even if it was just for those moments): the potential to become grounded and balanced was there. It was important at this stage for Alex to continue using meditation methods that he and his mum could enjoy together, until he felt comfortable practising on his own. The likelihood is *not* that he would be 'cured' of his ADHD, but with self-awareness and techniques to offload worries and feel calmer, he would allow himself to feel more settled on a more regular basis.

Grounding methods for children with ADHD

(For issues linked to root chakra, see table p.110)

Using the colour red

This colour is significant as it links to the root energy centre. We can 'artificially' encourage ourselves to feel more grounded by working with this colour. However it must be clear that you can't force someone to use this colour if they don't like it. Your logical head might think, 'Aha... my child will wear red socks today.' If you force something on children they will resist even more! Give them a choice of red or black or brown. If that fails and they go for another colour, so be it. Let it go and just

115

trust that your child's energy is choosing the right colour. The colour can be introduced in the form of socks, a cushion or a blanket to sit on or to use as a wrap.

During meditation, you can ask children to imagine the colour red. If they can't, then let them choose another colour instead. You will find that using the script from the colour meditation (see p.83) is a really useful way to bring colours into a meditation to help with grounding.

Hand mudras

Mudras are symbolic gestures that are used in some religions such as Buddhism or Hinduism. There is no religious intention suggested by using them here – for me it is simply a technique to help with focus and grounding. You may already have seen a common 'mudra' where a person sits cross-legged, with the tip of the first finger and thumb touching on each hand (see Figure 2 below). From a meditation and energetic perspective, this hand mudra is significant in helping your child to stay focused and grounded. Mudras help by influencing the energy flow through your body. They connect the physical body with the non-physical emotions, thoughts and spirit. They help to settle children's energy and are an excellent tool to use if they have had a busy day. You can also use them to help stay calm and focused as you lead your child through meditation.

Figure 2. The Ahamkara mudra

Figure 3. The Hakini mudra

If you are a bit sceptical of this, think about the hand positions you see people using naturally – or purposefully in the case of some politicians on TV. The Hakini mudra is used by many people in business, intentionally or not, as it helps overcome fear and timidity (Figure 3).

You can combine the Ahamkara mudra (Figure 2) with a simple meditation:

Ask your children to connect the tips of the thumb and first finger into the Ahamkara mudra (Figure 2).

Hold this hand position for 2–5 breaths.

Now ask them to move their thumb to the tip of their middle finger. Hold for 2–5 breaths.

Now ask them to move their thumb so it connects with the tip of their ring finger. Hold for 2–5 breaths.

Finally ask them to connect their thumb with the tip of their little finger. Hold for 2–5 breaths.

Depending on their age, for some children you may have to guide them to focus their attention (e.g. by asking them to notice the pressure of light/heavy touch of the finger tips, or the sound of the breath).

Then repeat the above but working backwards, moving the thumb from the little finger to the forefinger, holding each position for 2–5 breaths.

Using the breath with the body

The breath is a powerful tool for meditation and most people underestimate its significance. It is said that we can survive for weeks without food, days without water and minutes without air – so our breath is important.

Learning to focus on the breath (perhaps in combination with the hand mudra in the first instance) can help to settle your child's energy in that moment. That is why I teach adults to take their attention back to their breath when their mind drifts – the breath becomes their anchor point. You can do this with children too to ensure they pay it some attention. For children with ADHD, focusing is an issue. However they also have to breathe, so we can therefore use this as a tool! Counting the breath (silently to themselves) as they breathe in and out would be a good way for them to start – let their curiosity help them to notice how long/short the in- and out-breaths are in numbers. After practising this for a few breaths ask them to tell you what number they reached for the in-breath and the out-breath (see example p.45).

These methods help them to start to focus on one thing, and the breath is a powerful regulator of the body and energy.

Asking them to hold their breath for a count of 1 helps them to focus but it also helps to lengthen and calm the breath. They have to go at their own pace so even if they do this quite quickly, let them try. To lengthen the breath you might get them to hold the breath for a count of 2 if this helps slow things down. However, anything to do with the breath has to be done gradually to ensure your children don't feel anxious or agitated.

When you feel they have awareness of their breath, ask them to stop counting or holding it, as you are now going to ask them to combine it with movement. Ask your children to hold the Ahamkara mudra (see p.116) and when they breathe in – their thumb and first finger touch; when they breathe out – their fingers open. Keep repeating this for as many breaths as seems comfortable for the child: breathe in – fingers touch; breathe out – fingers open.

Then reverse it so that when they breathe in – fingers open, and when they breathe out – fingers close... and so on.

Now ask them which one they prefer and encourage them to practise this for 10 breaths whenever they can. Finish with them holding the fingers closed in the mudra position for 10 breaths.

The first cycle (breathe in – fingers closed, breathe out – fingers open) works with the root centre and helps their energy to have a clearer connection with the physical energy of the world around them, which helps them feel balanced and grounded. Opening the fingers with the out-breath gives a sense of release to any tension they hold in their energy. The second cycle (breathe in – fingers open, breathe out – fingers closed) works with the heart energy centre, which is all about balance. When they accept the air into their body with the fingers open, it has a balancing effect. When they breathe out with closed fingers, they are centring their energy with the earth – again aiding balance and helping them to ground their energy.

Working with crystals or stones

Crystals are excellent meditation aids simply because they help you to come into balance in a very subtle, natural way. If you are not sure how crystals work then perhaps this analogy will help.

If you walk into a cool room, your body responds to the temperature through some physiological responses to keep you warm (e.g. goose bumps). If the room is too warm, then your body responds but this time it will cool you down (e.g. sweat). Using crystals in meditation is like walking into the warm or cool room, where your energy responds to the energy of the crystal and you adjust to it. The energy that flows through a crystal is permanent and you are intuitively drawn to the crystal that works best with you.

Even though I have extensive experience of working with crystals, I have found that some children do not always choose grounding crystals, which my logical head suggests would work. Sometimes they are drawn to crystals like citrine that work with the solar plexus, a control centre, or blue quartz to work with the throat centre, which helps them to accept change or release emotions. Whatever crystal they choose is the right one. When your child has chosen a crystal, you can use it in a meditation (see stone meditation, p.62). If you are uncomfortable with the idea of crystals simply use a stone. Both crystals and stones come from the earth so their energy is very grounding. You can encourage your child to use the stone just as you would use the crystal in meditation, and for children with ADHD, this meditation tool can be very effective.

Ideas for grounding meditations

This is a type of meditation that focuses and encourages your contact with the ground and the earth. I sometimes use tree imagery in guided meditations, where the roots of the tree go deep down into the earth (sometimes with the breath), the bark of the tree is strong and supportive and the branches reach up to the light in the sky. The balancing effect of this meditation guides children through the grounding part of the roots moving into the earth before I guide them towards other parts of the tree. However you can use any kind of imagery that helps children to connect to the ground, such as walking in a forest or garden and being aware of plants and how they 'attach' to the ground.

Another way to encourage grounding in a meditation is to breathe through the feet – to encourage awareness of this part of the body. Ask children to tense their feet as they breathe in, relaxing them as they breathe out. You could guide your child to start at the feet and move up the legs (tensing/relaxing) to the base of the spine and then back down again, perhaps doing this several times.

Another option could be trying meditation whilst walking (eyes open) where your children focus on their feet, counting their steps then linking their breath to each step (breathe in – 2 steps, breathe out – 2 steps). You might then ask them to say how the ground feels. Is it hard (on concrete) or soft (on grass)? And, if possible, ask them to walk outside in their bare feet.

Aromatherapy oils and Bach flower remedies

Whilst they are natural, it is wise to be very careful when using aromatherapy oils with children as their respiratory systems are still developing. For the purposes of ADHD you may wish to use an oil such as sweet marjoram, which is relaxing, warming and grounding. For further information on using oils, see Chapter 4 (p.32), but if your child has any breathing problems, always check first with a qualified clinical aromatherapist before using oils.

Bach flower remedies were introduced to me by a fellow therapist, Linsey Denham, who is a qualified nurse with much experience of working in a children's hospital. The wonderful thing about Bach flower remedies is that they are safe to use with children and very easy to take. If your child tries them, they will either have a positive effect or no effect, whereby you can try another to find the correct one. Each remedy corresponds to an emotional state, and the remedies are blended together in a tincture that is taken in drinks to balance the person's energy and emotions. One flower remedy that springs to mind that may help with grounding is the clematis Bach flower remedy, however there are 38 to choose from and they can be helpful aids if you or your family feel overwhelmed trying to raise a child who has ADHD (you will find full details of Linsey's practice in the 'Resources' section, p.150).

Moving meditations

Sometimes we are actively grounding our energy even though we are unaware of this. Have you ever felt the need to get out into fresh air, go for a walk or a run? All of these activities are grounding. This is why 'ungrounded' people tend to move around a lot and can't stay still. In an unaware sense they are trying to naturally ground their energy. With awareness you can help your children to be more grounded by combining meditation with movement. Lots of physical exercise is important for children with ADHD as the more exercise they do, the more grounded they are. So walking, running and playing are important, especially in a natural environment with trees and fresh air. You could encourage your children to use activity to meditate, for example, with 1 minute spent walking, 1 minute spent running in a circle or on the spot, 1 minute spent running with arms out like an aeroplane, 1 minute spent walking and counting steps etc. These examples encourage them to ground their energy whilst combining this with focus and awareness.

Balancing methods for children with ADHD

(For issues linked to throat chakra, see table p.111)

Colour meditation and crystals

Colour and crystal meditations also work well for impulsive and inattentive children because they balance the throat chakra. For the colour meditation, see if they are drawn to the colours of this chakra (blue/turquoise). If your children chooses a different colour, don't panic but allow them to draw the one they are most comfortable with – we are working with children's intuition here, not logic.

Meditations using sound

Affirmations work with the vibration of sound. As you speak, you hear the words but energetically there is a vibration (physical as well as non-physical) that moves through your body. You make sound through your throat, which also links with the ears so it helps the balance between listening and talking.

A simple way to get your children to focus on their throats is for them to feel the vibration as they speak. Get them to gently hold their throats between their hands as they make the sound 'mmm'. Ask them to repeat this with their eyes closed. Now ask them to take a deep breath and try to make the 'mmm' sound as long as is comfortable for them. They can keep doing this a few more times.

They will feel the vibration in their hands, which encourages focus, and the sound helps to balance the energy here. Now when they are breathing out ask them to say the word 'haaaammmmmm'. This sound specifically vibrates to the balancing energy of the throat chakra. You can do this a few times (there may be a few giggles) but ask them to notice if the vibration feels different when they do this. If they have both hands around their throats (one at the top, one at the bottom) does the vibration move? Ask them to keep trying and noticing, which also encourages focus.

They can keep their hands on their throats, but now ask them to say 'I am' as 'Iiii... aaammm...' Keep repeating this 'I am' phrase and if you wish, ask them to complete the sentence with a word of their choice: 'I am calm', 'I am funny', 'I am smiling' and so on. You can demonstrate. See what happens and get them to keep practising with their favourite words.

If children are unable to speak or too shy to do this, ask them to follow all the actions above but silently and simply imagine that they are making this sound. Sometimes you can be silent, then you can speak, then it's their turn, then silence (just using the imagination) and so on. The body responds physiologically to our imagination so even if they are not speaking out loud, their bodies still feel the words and will be responding.

SINGING

What a wonderful way to work the throat chakra! You don't have to be in tune, but finding a song and singing it as well as you can is an excellent way to work this chakra. To create more power behind the singing you can encourage children to place their hands on their tummies and to squeeze all the air out to increase the volume as they sing.

TONING AND CHANTING

This involves making the same noise again and again with the purpose of simply vibrating sound and energy through the body via the throat chakra. Just use the vowels of the alphabet one at a time. Then get children to switch between the different vowels as they breathe out and tone the sound. So for example, you start with 'A' as in 'aaaaaa' then whilst making the sound you switch to 'E' as in 'eeeee'. Their faces will change to make the sound but also the vibration will change in their throats. Once they get used to the feeling of the sound vibration in their throats (through their hands) you can try it with the hands off and ask them to notice if they feel different sounds in other parts of their bodies. Have fun!

Case study with John

You may recall I talked earlier about how the left side of the brain involves more logical and practical thinking whilst the right side is the creative side. Let me explain how one little boy with ADHD taught me a valuable lesson.

John was diagnosed with ADHD at the age of seven. At first he was treated by an occupational health visitor as he was very clumsy and had very little spatial awareness. At the time they thought he had dyspraxia. The occupational therapist then asked for him to be referred to a consultant as she thought he may be slightly autistic. His eventual diagnosis was ADHD, for which he took medication to balance his symptoms, which included sleep issues. His mum commented that she thought some of his behaviour displayed signs of autism. Mum was a single parent bringing up both her son and daughter whilst living with her parents. She was also a full time student so she had lots of stress with studying and exams.

On meeting John I could see he was full of energy, bouncing on chairs and unable to focus on anything. I asked him to take part in an exercise with his mum and I tried to guide him through a simple colour meditation.

Before we started, he mentioned that he liked maths and numbers but hated anything creative or 'arty farty'. Did I listen to this? No – I did not! As a result I had an important lesson to learn.

I felt that he was a little unsure about taking part. I sensed that he was perhaps only there because his mum thought it was a good idea. I encouraged the mum to take part too. She was very easily distracted by her son's movements and his lack of interest in the meditation. The boy lay on the floor and I explained I was going to try and guide him through a colour meditation.

Meditation

We tried to do some relaxation with John lying on the floor, but he was quite restless. I asked him to think of a colour. He shrugged his shoulders: 'I can't think of any.' I asked him to think of his favourite colour – I got the same response. I asked him to just try and pretend and he said 'blue'. I realised that he had said this just to stop me from pestering him with this question! I asked him to think of the colour, surround himself in it and then eventually encouraged him to breathe it in. During this time he had moved to the sofa where he lay down and continued to kick his legs; he didn't seem to be paying much attention or following the guided meditation. We persevered for a few more minutes and as soon as I stopped he was off the sofa and into the next room, full of beans.

Observations

This was such an interesting case. I have to be honest and hold my hands up here and say that it did not work. But I know why. I reflected on this situation when I got home, realising that the guided meditation didn't have any effect at all. I told my husband about what had happened. With brilliant insight he suggested that as John wasn't interested in anything creative, then colour was not 'his thing'. Maybe I should have asked him to think of his favourite number instead as he liked maths so much. I realised the lesson I had learned. We have two sides to our brain: the logical, linear thinking side on the left, and the imaginative, creative side on the right. Some people are strongly logical or creative. Some people are balanced between the two. Meditation helps with this balancing of the left and right sides of the brain. I could have encouraged his imagination by using the number in the same way I had asked him to use a colour – to sit in the number or surround himself in it. Even though the imaginative challenge would have been the same, the use of a number, which he felt comfortable with, may have initiated the right side of the brain to be playful and active. This step would perhaps have started to encourage a balance between the left and right sides of the brain, rather then leaving it firmly centred in logic where he was comfortable.

My son who has ADHD has been listening to meditation CDs at bedtime for years. They help him to relax. He loves listening to them.

Parent

14. Children on the Autistic Spectrum

Our child is very sensitive in all senses. This, in turn, powers his mind on and on throughout the day at a supersonic speed. We found meditating helps him slow his mind down. It gives the mind a break of some sort ... helps slow him back down to a human speed.

Parent

I have discovered a wide variety of terms used to describe children on the autistic spectrum. Some parents take offence if their child with ADHD is seen as being on the autistic spectrum although it is a term I've heard educators use when referring to ADHD. Please be assured that I don't mean to cause offence to anyone, but in my research I discovered a large difference of opinion as to what constitutes 'autism'.

Children on the autistic spectrum range from those with very mild symptoms, which could be classed as ADHD (attention deficit hyperactivity disorder), to those who are high functioning (e.g. Asperger syndrome), to those demonstrating more extreme symptoms. My feelings are that children on the autistic spectrum are special and all quite different. In some respects their experiences and awareness of the world are poles apart from that of adults or other children.

My belief is that the energy of autistic children is not as grounded as ours, thus leaving their physical senses overexposed to the energy around us. Let me explain.

When you use a radio, you turn the dial, you can hear a hissing sound and then eventually the radio picks up the signal from the radio station and you have a clear signal with voices and music. This analogy demonstrates how most of us pick up the main signals of energy through our physical senses clearly and easily. Some autistic children find it difficult to tune into these signals so therefore seem to be stuck between 'stations' and all they perceive is the hissing sound (interference). Then there are some children who are not stuck between signals, but can pick up many more signals than an ordinary person; just like some types of radio can pick up signals from countries thousands of miles away. Therefore they have more information to process than you or I, and their perception of the world is quite different from ours.

Our physical senses act as filters that help us connect to and make sense of the world. We see light but we can also feel it on our skin if it's warm like the sun. Our bodies and physical senses are designed to cope with the world around us and to keep us in a balanced state (homeostasis). So if you were to sit in the sun too long, or without protection, you might become dehydrated and have to drink water or get out of the sun as your skin started to burn. I believe that some autistic children have filters that are more open than ours, so they don't filter out a lot of the information and are very sensitive to their environment, and particularly to changes in that environment.

For example, if we see a light bulb, our senses detect the light and perhaps the heat depending on how close we are to it. We see this light as most people do and it seems normal. However, autistic children may be much more aware of this 'information' and to them it seems more like a 600 watt or even 6000 watt light bulb. For us, such a bright light would be unbearable and we would turn our faces from it, shield our eyes or find a way to switch it off. We do what we have to do to cope with our environment. Autistic children are reacting to their environment and doing what they can to cope and protect themselves from this overload on their sensory organs.

Sound is another example we can use to help us understand what it may be like for autistic children. We know how an ambulance siren passing in the street can hurt our ears. Autistic children can be very sensitive to certain sounds. Similar to how dogs react to a dog whistle, which most human beings can't hear. Autistic children would do what we would in those circumstances, and cover their ears or try to get away from the sound. They will do what they can to cope and stay in balance, even if these are sounds we adults can't hear.

Imagine that sometimes you feel dizzy when you stand up (a head rush) and the world goes blurry for a moment and you think you're going to fall. What do you do? You put out your hands and arms either side to steady your balance. It's what a tightrope walker does to help stay connected to the rope. I believe that when autistic children flap their hands on either side of them, they are telling us that their energy feels ungrounded and unsafe. It's difficult to know for sure, but I believe they do this to steady and ground their energy. As adults all we see is strange behaviour that does not fit in with our perceptions of how people should behave. But we don't walk in the shoes of these children so we can't know exactly what they're thinking or feeling; all we can do is let them do what it takes to help them feel more balanced at that time.

Another example I might use to help you understand my theories on autistic children is that of the cat world. I have two cats and, as you may know, cats have a super-sensitive ability to pick up sound, vibration and wind currents through their whiskers and sense of smell. When they come into their home, they spend a lot of time rubbing against furniture and people to mark their territory, and they use this to help orientate themselves in their environment. When they 'know' through their super-senses where everything is, they are settled and feel safe. If we decide to add a new piece of furniture, cats are fascinated or fearful and spend time rubbing against it so that it has their smell and they can accept it into their world. Autistic children can be super-sensitive to their environment like this. Perhaps we could compare their repeated behaviour to cats rubbing against the same pieces of furniture, helping children to feel connected to their environment and therefore safe. Perhaps that's why some autistic children have tantrums when things are moved or taken away, as to them this is a major change in their world. That item helped them feel grounded and connected to their environment and without it they feel destabilised.

These examples are to help you understand how the environment we experience is different in some ways for children on the autistic spectrum – not only what they see (shielding eyes), touch (dislike of clothing/trying to be naked), smell (odours), sound (covering ears) and taste (food intolerances), but also to the energy of others. However, not all children will behave identically as they are unique – each with their own place on a spectrum of energy that they share with us.

How children respond to negative energy

The founders of the Son-Rise Program in the USA developed their programme so that they could 'reach their son' (see p.11). I've spoken to parents of children on the autistic spectrum and some have talked about the difficulty in connecting with their children emotionally. I've listened to parents describe their children as living in their own world as if they were aliens in a foreign land. Perhaps through the examples I have given you can start to understand why children respond in this way.

When we (adults) are in balance, our energy is calm, peaceful and joyful. Imagine that when our energy is calm it is as soft as a cosy blanket. If we're thinking negative thoughts, feeling angry, emotional, anxious, nervous or stressed then our energy changes. It feels prickly or jaggy, like a hedgehog. Perhaps you can see how your children, particularly if they are on the autistic part of the spectrum, will sense this. They respond to the energy of others and will react accordingly. Even if you think you're 'hiding' these negative feelings or suppressing them, children will still sense and react to them.

I believe that *all* children pick up on our energy in these subtle sensitive ways and that's why it can be terrifying for a young child to experience an angry person. For autistic children, they pick up on that negative energy even if the anger or frustration isn't directed at them, for example, if you've had a bad day at work and have come home with all that bad energy hanging around in your system. When I was first introduced to working with children on the autistic spectrum I was very excited about ideas and theories I had to help them stay calm, focused and help balance their energy. Whilst some of the methods have had a positive and interesting influence, for example, in helping children to settle and relax at bedtime, I also noticed that the parents were being 'taught' by their children how to become calmer and more peaceful. In other words, parents teaching their children how to relax, meditate and feel calmer also start to benefit by feeling more relaxed themselves. Children learn by example and respond to the 'sea of energy' around them.

Autistic children are unique

I do not for one minute think you can suddenly transform yourself and your feelings of anger and frustration to a state of peace and tranquillity.

It takes practice, practice and more practice and the first step is to acknowledge these feelings and accept them.

One of the insights I received in my own meditation practice is that autistic children are very special indeed. But it's not so much about changing them or making them fit into our lives, but rather that to be around them we have to slow down, be calmer and more 'in the moment'.

A really important point to make for people with autistic children is to approach them with the awareness that they are unique. When I've met parents with an autistic child, they often seem to seek a single, clear set of guidance notes – a blueprint or map of the difficult situation they are in. I don't judge people for feeling like that as it must be absolutely exhausting for them. However there is no map. I hope this book contains a few signposts, but some of them will not apply to you. Hopefully my advice will encourage you to discover your own map so that you can reach your children and guide them along their unique path, so you can walk it together. Sometimes you'll be guiding them and sometimes they'll be guiding you.

If you've never come across meditation and energy in the form of healing, it can be difficult to accept some of these theories and concepts. But if you consider that we share energy just as we share the air that we breathe, then perhaps you will begin to observe your children through a different pair of eyes. With awareness, you might find that your children are trying their best to cope with a very demanding and sometimes extremely frightening environment.

Case study with Matt

Matt was aged ten and had been diagnosed with Asperger syndrome a few years prior to this. In his mother's words, 'It was a fight to get the authorities and the school to recognise that Matt was not being a difficult child but had autism.' Until the parents could get this diagnosis, they had no help from the authorities and were at their wits end, understandably. Matt had a brother (Peter) who did not have this diagnosis. Matt was not on any medication but I had managed to encourage the whole family to try Bach flower remedies (see p.146).

Meditation

First visit – I was unsure of what to expect. This was the first autistic child I had visited. His mum chatted to me about the history of Matt's behavioural development. After a few minutes Matt was keen for me to see his bedroom, which had just been decorated. With his mum's permission I went up to his room. Matt liked to talk a lot. I tried some meditation with him directly, asking if he wanted to try. 'Ok.' So far so good.

I asked him to think of a colour. Matt had been lying down but I noticed that he fidgeted a lot. He sat up and asked if he could draw the colour. I realised that Matt had to see the colour in order to think about it (at first). He drew a few colours with pencils on a piece of paper then lay back down. I guided him through some very quick relaxation by tensing and releasing his muscles. His attention span was short so it was important for me not to waste time. His first colour was green – he continued with this and could feel it in his chest (this is the colour of the heart chakra energy centre and is a balancing point between physical and non-physical energy). The colour then changed to purple (the crown energy centre at the top of the head which is all to do with 'spiritual/ big picture' stuff). When I asked Matt to breathe in the colour green, he became uncomfortable and didn't want to take it down into his feet. We stopped there and then Matt demonstrated his new skills on his first musical instrument – the school recorder. It was time for me to leave but as I was saying goodbye, Matt gave me a big hug and a smile. Many autistic children don't show affection and Matt seemed to fall into that category. It was interesting to see how things had changed in that first visit.

Second visit (a few weeks later) – I managed to spend a little more time with the family. Life seemed to be quite a whirlwind in the household so I wasn't able to collect any observations about how Matt had been after my first visit. This time I brought Matt and his brother some crystals. I asked them to choose a crystal. Matt chose amethyst, which links with the crown chakra, and his brother chose tiger's eye, which links with the solar plexus. We tried some very simple meditations, in which Mum joined in, where the boys spent some time with their eyes closed just touching the crystals with their fingers – feeling the surface, weight, warmth/coolness and so on. I talked them through this and could see that Matt was a little restless, but we managed to continue for about 10 minutes. I advised his mum that this crystal was particularly useful for placing under a pillow to help sleep, as she mentioned that he had sleep problems. She also mentioned that he loved crystals and had quite a collection in his room! So guess where I went after the meditation? Back to Matt's room so he could show me his crystals. I asked Mum if it was okay to try some Reiki healing with him. I had Matt sitting up and, without touching, I placed my hands close to his head (where healing normally begins). Within moments he turned around and asked if I could do Reiki on his feet instead. I obliged. Then we continued through the chakras. I noticed that Matt was silent for a minute then would say, 'Can't feel anything.' Then I would move on to the next chakra. I felt that he was telling me that it was time to move on and that the energy centres had absorbed as much as they could that day. I suggested to his mum that she perhaps learn Reiki. It is a great way to practise self-healing and meditation, and is useful for tired and anxious parents, as well as supporting both her sons and particularly Matt at bedtime when he found it difficult to sleep. She agreed and came along to one of my Reiki classes.

Feedback

I advised Mum that she should not be disheartened about how long Matt could meditate for. A minute can be a miracle sometimes, though I know as a parent you have higher hopes! This might not seem much to start with but for a child who never sits still or asks lots of questions all the time, a minute of meditation is very encouraging.

Matt's mum replied, 'I think Matt was definitely more chilled than usual on Friday evening. I went out for a walk with him and the dog to look for conkers and he seemed relaxed. Also, I don't know if it's the remedies or not but I've not felt as tearful so that's positive!'

After Mum came to learn Reiki she told me:

> I've not done any self-healing yet but when I got back on
> Saturday after the course, Matt asked me to 'do it to him',
> which I did when he was under his bed lying down watching
> TV. Just a short session head to feet but then he asked me to

do it again. I also did a session on Peter in his bed just as he was going to sleep. Matt listened to the meditation track 'Tree of Protection' (see 'Resources' for details, p.148) to fall asleep last night. Matt does seem to be more 'lovey dovey' – for want of a better way of explaining it! – after the Reiki. He came into our bed one morning this week for a lovely cuddle and he hasn't done that for a long time. I'm still taking the Bach remedies (just me) four or more times a day. We are so grateful for the sessions you have had with us so far.

Meditation

Third visit – I decided to take along my singing bowls and Tibetan bells. I let the boys play with them, making noises and showing how to create a sound from them (it's similar to how we make a noise by wetting our finger and running it around the rim of a glass). The boys loved making a noise! I offered on this occasion to do a Reiki healing with the mum. The boys agreed to go to their rooms, though mum said there would be noise once they started arguing. However within 5 minutes of starting the healing the house was silent. During the healing, Matt came into our room for a minute to pick something up, came up to his mum and kissed her on the forehead. Mum told me afterwards that this was something he rarely did now.

Feedback

> Thanks so much for the visit on Friday – I feel we all really benefited from it. We are already halfway through our Bach remedies too as we're all taking them and even managing to get my sceptical hubby to take them too!

I also suggested that they try some regular online meditations through a free resource I had found (see 'Resources' for details, p.149). This was a programme of forty days with a different meditation for each day. The tutor, Susan Kaiser-Greenland, offered a short 4-minute meditation for younger children and longer meditations for older children. Mum decided to try these, so they downloaded them on to their mp3 player and listened to them daily:

We're trying regular online meditations and, just to let you know how we are getting on, I'm doing the shorter one with Matt and the longer one with Peter. So far we're doing them at every bedtime and the boys are more or less drifting off to sleep pretty quickly after we finish, but the good thing is I still feel fairly alert after it so I don't feel I have to nod off myself at their earlier bedtime.

That's Matt finished his forty days of meditations now. I tried holding his feet and he let me do it some nights but didn't want me to do it on others. We are having a nice time relaxing and sitting quietly, but that's a good thing as at bedtime Matt's mind is often racing and he wants to talk.

Meditation

Fourth visit – I asked them to come to my home as I wanted to see how the boys reacted in a different environment. I have two cats and lots of crystals! Matt was fascinated by the house so he was exploring every inch of it – up and downstairs. I noticed that although he was very energetic, when he petted the cats he was very gentle and talked to them too. I asked Mum and Peter if they wanted to try a meditation. Matt was not interested in this but wanted to draw instead. I gave him some paper and a pen. I was playing my Tibetan bell music and as soon as Matt heard it he stopped in his tracks (remember, he had been racing around) and stood listening to it for a minute. I started to take Mum and Peter through a short guided meditation and Matt lay on the floor next to me quietly drawing. In fact he produced a full cartoon feature during that time and didn't make a sound. As soon as the meditation stopped he became more lively but slightly calmer than he had been when they had first arrived.

Observations

I noticed a couple of things on this visit. First of all, cats are very sensitive to strangers and my cats are friendly but usually can't stand children! Yet the most sensitive cat was quite happy for Matt to pet him. I think both boy and cat were appreciating each other's 'sensitive' energy. The music had a profound effect on Matt and seemed to help him stay focused and calm. During this time his mum was meditating and her calmer energy (she is quite an energetic person) seemed to help him stay calm too.

Top tips when working with an autistic child

Rachel still enjoys meditation and it's also given us another way of being close and connecting without physical contact (sensory issues mean we don't have many hugs or touch).

Parent

Bring your energy into balance first

It's really tempting to dive in and try using these methods first with your children, but if you don't feel calm then it will be more challenging for you both. As a parent or carer with an autistic child, you are probably, understandably, quite stressed. In order to get the most benefit out of trying meditation, it's really important that you feel calm or at least try to acknowledge and process your feelings. Try some of the self-awareness methods (see Chapter 8, p.72) so you can become aware of the moment, your breath and how you are feeling. This simple act can help you to unwind and calm down. Try this on your own to start with even if it's just lying in bed at night. Once you get a feel for it, start to practise it at work or in the shower, at the bus stop or a red traffic light, making a cup of tea – and eventually in the company of your children. If you find that trying this method brings up lots of feelings and emotions, then let them out. They will not go away and I would also suggest writing them down and shredding or burning them afterwards, which may help lighten the load and your energy. Repeat as often as necessary.

Stay grounded

Most people feel overwhelmed when they feel ungrounded. All parents feel overwhelmed when a child enters their lives as it takes so much energy. If you can stay grounded then you will find it easier to focus, concentrate and cope. Try the grounding techniques, which use visualisations that connect your feet to the ground (see p.120). Whilst you're practising self-awareness with your children, if you feel wobbly in any way, just tense your feet and relax them with the breath to ground yourself again.

Take a back seat

Adults feel compelled to organise children – and I agree that children need boundaries – but unless they are physically causing harm to themselves or others, just let them be. Sit back, with self-awareness, and just observe your children with no judgement. If you are judging them and wishing they were different, then honour those feelings and breathe them away. Even if the feelings become quite intense, use your breath to acknowledge, accept then release them. This is a powerful, releasing step in your own energy and self-awareness. Continue to just watch your children with the intention of letting go for those few moments.

Work from the heart centre

This energy centre in our chest represents accepting ourselves for who we are, accepting those we share life with and accepting life itself. The energy of the heart is unconditional acceptance. When we try to control, we use the energy of our solar plexus and by doing so we use up a lot of mental, emotional and physical energy that drains us. You will know if you're trying to control energy through the solar plexus as it will feel physically tense. Instead, try to imagine a smile painted on your chest. Or simply think about this area – notice it. Focus on the journey of your breath into your chest and imagine that each out-breath moves out of your chest and surrounds you like a soft blanket of energy. As you move away from the control centre of the solar plexus to the softer energy of the heart centre, you empower yourself with the wisdom of inner peace.

Identify key issues

What are the main issues that cause stress? Is your child demanding attention, or not listening, not sleeping or has odd or repetitive behaviour. Does the behaviour need to change (e.g. if harmful)? Identify the key issues and break them down into 'what, who, why, when'. Then with a little creativity, think up some baby steps you can take to see 'how' things can change, but try to channel your creativity not by thinking logically, but thinking creatively (see Chapter 8).

Food issues

Are there food issues that cause difficult behaviour? Can you map your children's moods and behaviour and record what they eat and when? I recommend an excellent book about nutritional issues in the 'Resources' section (p.149) about how food can affect your children.

Go outside

I have spoken to many parents who tell me that they spend too much time indoors to avoid interactions with other people who may judge them or their children. For every human being, it's imperative to spend time in the fresh air – in the garden, a park or by the sea. Time spent in nature is one of the most grounding and balancing steps you can take for both you and your children.

Singing bowls

I've noticed that these have a very calming affect on children with autism and I think it's because the tones of the bowls resonate and vibrate with the chakras of the body. Simply playing this music in the background and/or meditating to it may help you and your child feel calmer.

Crystals

These are very useful tools to use in meditation and for balancing. Simply holding the crystal or having it in your pocket will help. Meditating with it is also helpful, but you don't have to do this for it to work. Remember to choose a crystal for you and your partner too!

Red socks

The feet are the most tactile part of us that touches the ground, hence why they are important in grounding our energy. Try to stand with both your feet flat on the ground and the weight evenly distributed between them, or when sitting have your feet flat on the floor. Wear red socks, slippers or shoes to help with grounding (maybe your children will enjoy this too), as this is the colour of the root energy centre. Or try spending time holding or rubbing your children's feet if they enjoy this. All these methods can help with grounding.

Relaxation

Try the progressive muscle relaxation methods (e.g. tensing muscles and relaxing them, see p.49) to encourage your children to sense their bodies. If they are happy for you to touch them, you can gently touch the part of the body you are asking them to tense then relax.

Routines

I've noticed that some children on the autistic spectrum like routines. This structure makes them feel safe in what they perceive as an unsafe world. If you can schedule a meditation practice of any kind – morning, daytime, evening – this encourages them to try meditation in a routine. Try to join in too as you will benefit from the regular practice. It could be anything from 10 relaxing breaths to a full colour meditation.

Breath and the body

If your children are happy trying meditation with the breath (see p.55) then ask them to point to an area of their body that they wish to start with and then work up or down the body from there. Take time to do a few breaths at that part of the body before moving on. Ask your children to tell you where they want to go next. What you are doing here is working with the energy of each chakra and helping them to focus.

BREATHING THROUGH THE FEET

Combining this part of the body with the breath helps you and your children to stay or become grounded. You may use imagery with this (like roots of a plant) or a tactile approach (tensing and relaxing muscles) to help your children ground their energy.

Grounding mudra

If you turn to Chapter 13 on working with ADHD (see p.116), you will see some hand positions called 'mudras' which are very useful to learn for meditation and grounding.

So you now have lots of 'tools' and tips to try! My advice is just to try one thing to start with so you learn what works and what doesn't. You may find that children love doing one activity, but when you try it again they hate it. This is good, as it indicates a change in their energy. Choose a different method or technique and see how you progress from there. In meditation, there is no right or wrong experience. Please adapt any of these methods to suit your own unique situation by trusting your imagination and intuition.

Spectrum of life

As I gathered my research on this subject, what struck me is that I started to notice and observe some of these autistic behaviours in so-called 'normal' people (including myself), all be it on a milder scale. For example, a need for order and routine, anxiety when routines are changed, poor sleep, inability to sit still or focus, emotionally distant, unable to socialise, only interested in science/maths/computers and so on. Consider this: all children and adults exist on a spectrum of energy. We are all linked to each other and experience this connection to the spectrum of life in our own unique way. It's food for thought.

15. Calming Methods for You

*I have meditated with my aunt and grandma since I was twelve ...
now in my forties, my ten- and fifteen-year-olds are meditating with
me daily. My reason for doing this is that it helps a lot with daily life's
tribulations! I feel we should all meditate when we can.*

Parent

Reiki

In addition to teaching meditation, I also teach complementary
therapies. One of these therapies is the healing system of Reiki.

During the first level of Reiki training (which helps you to practise
self-healing and to heal with family and friends) you learn about the
Reiki Principles. Whether or not you are trained in Reiki, this is a useful
tool to use to help you stay calm as a parent or educator, or simply as an
adult trying to cope with the challenges of life.

The phrase 'Just for today' is to encourage you to be in this moment.
Simply focusing on your breath first, then breathing into your chest 'Just
for today' and breathing out 'I will not worry' will help in a number of
ways:

- It will help you to focus on your breath
- It will help you to stay in the moment
- It will help you to acknowledge your worry more clearly
- It will help you to accept this worry
- It will then help you to release this worry (and its associated
  feelings and thoughts, which can be very draining on your energy)

When I teach students to use these phrases for meditation, it helps them be in the moment, to feel calm and to let go of negative thoughts and emotions. Sometimes we just focus on the phrase that means most to them or sometimes we use all of them, one after the other. Even if you think that these phrases don't relate to you, just sit down and try connecting them to your breath as I've described above and notice how you feel (self-awareness) as you do this. If you stay with one phrase for several breaths it will give you time to adjust and become aware of how you feel and respond to that statement.

The Reiki Principles (as I use them):

Just for Today,
I will not worry.
Just for Today,
I will not be angry.
Just for Today,
I will speak truthfully.
Just for Today,
I will love and respect all.
Just for Today,
I will feel gratitude for all.

A personal story...

I was teaching these to some school teachers and one of them was quite sceptical about the benefit of these words and using them in meditation with the breath. She told me an interesting story, which I thought I would share:

The following week after the meditation class, she left her house for work only to discover that all her neighbours' bins had been left behind her car after the council's rubbish men had been to empty them. One by one, she had to move fourteen wheelie bins out of the way to drive her car to work. By the time she'd removed the last one she was seething with anger. As she drove her car to work, hands gripping the steering wheel, she composed an angry letter to the council in her head. Then she stopped at a traffic light. For some reason she remembered the Reiki Principles. She decided to repeat one to herself with the breath. Then she noticed that the phrase she was using was 'Just for this moment, I will feel calm.' So she continued on with this for the rest of the journey to work. When she arrived she realised that she no longer felt angry. She did not want to write the letter either, but most importantly of all she realised that had she stepped into the classroom in this rage, her energy would have negatively affected the children. Children are like mirrors, so when they pick up energy like anger, they respond. The teacher realised that the whole day could have descended into chaos. As a result of using the phrase with her breath, she found herself to be calmer and the day with the children was a peaceful one.

This story demonstrates the importance of practising something to help you feel calmer. As you feel calmer, your children will reflect this calmness back to you.

16. Beyond Meditation – Methods and Tools

Although you bought this book with the intention of teaching children mindful activities and meditation, try to see it as a stepping stone rather than the end goal. This book offers you some useful ideas and suggestions but there are other options (some similar to meditation) that might be beneficial or even more suitable for the needs of your children. I have suggested these options here.

Moving meditation

Meditation is often perceived as a seated, stationary practice but there are some forms of moving meditation that can be just as effective and, for some children, more suitable. The intention of moving meditation is the same as still meditation – the development of self-control and awareness, helping to focus the mind and bringing the body back into balance physically, mentally and emotionally. In moving meditation, this awareness combines the breath and the body but it relates specifically to movement. If children are finding it impossible to sit still long enough to enjoy meditation, then a moving meditation might be the answer. It could even be the starting point that helps them to eventually sit in a still meditation position in the future – if this is of benefit to them.

Moving meditations I would suggest include qigong, tai chi and yoga for children. Details of these are listed below though I would suggest that you engage the help of a qualified teacher:

Qigong (chi kung) was once described to me as the 'warm up' for tai chi and originated in China hundreds of years ago. It combines awareness of the breath and movements to help the flow of 'air energy' through the energy system (body of mind, emotions and physical elements). It is practised widely throughout China and is viewed as a supportive practice for reducing stress – working with the breath and the diaphragm.

Tai chi is a practice originating in China and dating back many centuries. Whilst we in the West view it as the ideal 'low-impact exercise' it helps develop an awareness of personal energy (*chi* as it is called in this case) that is beneficial physically, emotionally and mentally, as it combines breath work with physical movement. Tai chi is seen as the preparatory stage for those wishing to practise martial arts.

Yoga is another ancient practice that comes from India. The word itself means 'union' and yoga is part of the Ayurvedic practice of health in India, which sees the person as energy that is influenced by diet, exercise and the environment (internal and external). Although it is viewed as a physical exercise in the West, it has a cleansing and beneficial effect on the energy centres of the body that help it to come into balance physically, mentally and emotionally. It can be a more dynamic movement than perhaps the other forms of moving meditation.

Meditation tools

Mandalas are what I call a meditation tool. They are linked to many cultures that practise meditation. The mandala is a black and white geometric circular design, which can then be coloured in by children with awareness – awareness of the colours they choose and how they feel as they colour. It is almost as if you can deposit your feelings and thoughts into the mandala as you colour it. The word 'mandala' means 'sacred circle' and the process of colouring it in is said to help bring balance and release energy blockages (in the West we would call this releasing fears and frustrations). It is a wonderful mindful activity to do with children, observing them as they complete it (be aware of the colours they choose as this might indicate which chakras are coming into balance).

You can also ask children to notice how they feel as they colour it in. They do not need to tell you – they just need to be aware of what they are feeling as they colour in the mandala. After it has been completed children can gently gaze at the mandala, connecting their breath to it and releasing any unhappy feelings into it. Afterwards they can choose to keep the mandala (if it makes them feel safe or happy) or let go of the mandala by cutting it up or shredding it (if it makes them feel sad or scared). It is a very healing tool and there are websites where you can download free ones to use (see 'Resources', p.150). If you are completing it yourself, it's a good idea to use your non-dominant hand in order to tap into your inner energy. This is not necessary with children, though you might give them the choice of which hand they want to use – depending on what they want to express (feelings or thoughts).

Reiki is a form of energy healing that originates from Japan and it's something I've taught for years (including a few children – though it's mainly adults who come to learn). It encourages a meditative approach when practising self-healing, which is the first level of Reiki healing. Plus the attunement process in Reiki 1 (like a deep meditation that helps rebalance the energy) is a life-long skill. Some of the principles in Reiki – 'Just for today, I will not be angry' (see Chapter 15) – can be used in a meditation and provide a lovely affirmation or mantra to help with focus and balance. I have taught a few children Reiki which, their parents have told me, has brought them some peace. It would be useful for you as the adult to learn Reiki to help keep your own energy balanced and to help create a peaceful environment for your child to meditate within.

Indian head massage – I also teach this healing therapy which is primarily seen as a clothed massage technique. To receive and practise Indian head massage is extremely soothing and can be quite meditative too; it has a positive and balancing effect on the energy centres. Practised throughout society and families in India, it's a nurturing and bonding experience which children can learn to do for themselves, or which you can learn to practise on each other and other family members. It's a very simple therapy to learn and again another life-long skill to help de-stress. I've heard from some parents with children who are autistic that they particularly like being massaged – this would be a good one to try.

Mudras – I first discovered these a few years ago. Whilst the term 'mudra' can refer to body, eye and hand positions that help balance energy and support meditation practice, it's only the hand positions I have used with good effect in meditation. The position of the fingers and hands and how you connect with this during meditation can be used to balance your energy. Mudras are seen as spiritual gestures and are often seen in Indian dance, but also many Buddhist statues have their hand positions held within a particular mudra, which will have a spiritual meaning. I have found a few of them to be very effective to help my beginners' classes settle down into meditation, and one in particular that we use to help with focus and concentration (see p.116).

Crystals – I also find that crystals can be very comforting for children. This is based on the idea that crystals are energy (remember what we said about the universe consisting of energy and that our energy interacts with the energy of our environment, see Chapter 5). Crystals are seen as little pockets of energy wrapped up in this crystallized form. We use them in the technical world – clear quartz crystals have electrical energy potential and are used in quartz clocks. The same applies to us, as our own energy is positively affected by crystals. The important consideration if using crystals in meditation is to let your children choose for themselves; they will always choose the right one as their energy attracts the energy of the crystal that is most suited to them. If you let them choose, then you might consider researching the crystal and no doubt will learn a lot about your children (and their energy) if you do so.

Your children will find that as they hold a crystal or have it somewhere on their body (in a pocket for example) it helps to bring their energy back into balance. It's a useful meditation tool as it does not require you to think about it but simply to have it in the meditation space.

Bach flower remedies – Flower remedies were discovered by Dr Bach in the 1930s and are used extensively to help balance emotional energy. There are 38 different flower remedies to match different emotions. They are easily taken as a tincture in drinks and have no harmful effects on children. They are an excellent way for adults and children to support themselves emotionally, especially when going through times of change, such as moving house, going to school or sitting exams.

Kinesiology – This therapy tests the body's muscle and energy response to certain questions. It's an excellent way to detect nutritional allergies or imbalances in the body and can help the body to rebalance energies. The therapist lightly touches the person's arm as they ask certain questions and when the muscle 'switches off' the body has answered, so the answer does not come through the conscious mind. This therapy may be helpful in determining if your children have any nutritional issues that are affecting their energy levels and behaviour.

Colour therapy – This involves working with a trained therapist who will use different colours to identify issues and treat a person's unbalanced energy. By choosing certain colours, the therapist can identify which energy centres need healing. Most children respond well to colour, so this is an easy way to help children communicate what they are feeling and where they need support. For less imaginative children, the tactile nature of the colours helps them to choose the one they like or dislike the most.

Reflexology – This therapy involves touching the feet or hands and releasing energy blockages in the body through gentle massage. The energy lines in the body come to a point in different locations in the feet or hands. By stimulating or calming these energy points we can feel more balanced. As the therapy involves touching the feet and the feet are linked to the root chakra, this is an excellent way to help grounding and balance if your child is finding it difficult to concentrate and focus.

EFT (emotional freedom technique) – This therapy is easy to learn and can be a very effective way to help deal with strong emotions. It involves tapping certain energy points on the body whilst focusing on the strong emotion (or whatever thought is causing the upset). Tapping allows us to release the blockage and for the strong feelings of distress to reduce.

Resources

Further resources from Lorraine Murray

To contact Lorraine Murray with any questions or suggestions you can email her at info@ilovefgt.com.

To find out more about the CDs and courses Lorraine Murray offers, including Calm Kids – Teach Children Meditation (beginner and professional level), courses in Usui and Karuna Reiki, Indian head massage and meditation for adults, please visit www.ilovefgt.com or www.teachchildrenmeditation.com.

For useful articles, meditation ideas and more on Facebook and Twitter:
www.facebook.com/#!/teachchildrenmeditation
www.twitter.com/#!/meditation4kids

Guided meditation CDs for children

The following were all created by Lorraine Murray and are available from the website www.ilovefgt.com/shop:

Crystal Clear – a crystal and meditation CD for children aged 5+.

Chill Zone – breath meditation for teenagers to cope with stress.

Calm Kids – ADHD – a series of grounding meditations to help children with ADHD.

Calm Kids – Asperger syndrome – a series of meditations to help with sleep issues and grounding.

Calm Kids – Autism – a series of meditations to help with grounding, anxiety and balancing the energy centres.

Free meditation resources for children

The following are by Susan Kaiser-Greenland and are available from www.talkshoe.com:
Mindfulness for Teenagers
Mindfulness for Children

Music for meditation

For light music for guided meditations try the instrumentalist Deuter: *Reiki – Hands of Light, Buddha Nature, Earth Blue* or *Wind and Mountain*.

For singing bowl music (useful for focus and breath meditations or working with ADHD and autism) try Deuter, *Nada Himalaya*.

For music with a steady drumbeat (useful for grounding and balance) try the musician Anugama, *Shamanic Dreaming*.

Further reading

Donna Eden, *Energy Medicine*, Piatkus Books, 2008.

Adele Faber & Elaine Mazlish, *How to Talk So Kids Will Listen and Listen So Kids Will Talk*, Piccadilly Press, 2001.

Shakti Gawain, *Creative Visualization*, New World Library, 2002.

Judy Hall, *The Crystal Bible: A Definitive Guide to Crystals*, Godsfield Press, 2003.

Thich Nhat Hanh, *Anger: Buddhist Wisdom for Cooling the Flames*, Rider, 2001.

Eric Harrison, *Teach Yourself to Meditate*, Piatkus Books, 1994.

Dr Natasha Campbell-McBride, *Gut and Psychology Syndrome: Natural Treatment for Autism, ADD/ADHD, Dyslexia, Dyspraxia, Depression, Schizophrenia*, Medinform Publishing, 2010.

Sami Timimi, *Naughty Boys: Anti-social Behaviour, ADHD and the Role of Culture*, Palgrave Macmillan, 2005.

Therapies

Therapist organisations

UKRF – professional association of Reiki teachers and practitioners: www.reikifed.co.uk

Kinesiology Federation – for practitioners in muscle testing (useful for allergies): www.kinesiologyfederation.co.uk

Bach Centre – professional register of Bach Flower Practitioners: www.bachcentre.com

IFPA – professional association of aromatherapists: www.ifparoma.org

Therapists

Liz Bell – crystal therapist: lizrbell@talktalk.net

Linsey Denham – children and Bach flower remedies: www.bachflowerconsultsonline.com

Roushan Martens – EFT practitioner (emotional freedom technique): http://www.sulastherapies.co.uk

Agnes T. McCluskey – colour therapist: www.colourenergytherapies.co.uk

Lorraine Murray – Usui and Karuna Reiki: www.ilovefgt.com

Dee Taylor –autism (adults), aromatherapist and Reiki: www.deetaylortherapies.co.uk

Eleanor Taylor – kinesiologist (muscle testing): www.eleanortaylortherapies.co.uk

Anne Young – children and aromatherapy: www.scents-of-wellbeing.co.uk

Other websites of interest

Free mandalas:
http://yogainmyschool.com/2009/12/23/mandala-magic-teaching-kids-about-meditation
http://www.mandala-4u.com/en/start.html

Hand mudras – www.eclecticenergies.com/mudras/introduction.php

Jack draws anything – how a child can make a difference – www.jackdrawsanything.com

The Son-Rise Program – www.autismtreatmentcenter.org
Yoga for kids – www.yogainmyschool.com/category/kids
Power of your child's Imagination – www.imageryforkids.com
Emotional intelligence – www.theiamprogram.com

Acknowledgements

I would like to thank so many people for helping me reach this point in my life of writing a book. Who would have believed it! The loving thanks must be extended first to my mum for persevering with me, as an unruly teenager, to teach me meditation in the first place; to my teacher Kim McManus who helped me develop my teaching skills; to all my friends for believing in me, but especially to Sandie Lowrie, Dee Taylor, Linda Rodgers, Jackie Cohen, Tania Gillespie, Jen Baxter, Kiwi Kaz, Audrey Hird, Linsey Denham, Brenda Bartel, Jane Burgess, Hazel Greenhalgh, Lorna Kellock, Anne Scott and Lesley Brannen.

Thanks also to Sheila Laing the head teacher who was brave enough to let me try meditation with children in the first place. Thanks to the children of Forthview Primary School in Edinburgh for helping me learn how to teach meditation to kids. Thanks to Lisa Murray for all her sage advice. Thanks to all those on our Facebook page who gave us the most inspirational quotes (that you'll read in this book). Thanks to the families I worked with who experience ADHD and autism – you were wonderful. Heartfelt thanks to my nephew Ryan and Al Pal for letting me test meditation ideas with them. Much gratitude to Sally Polson my editor who has done a sterling job of guiding me through the labyrinth of book editing and the publishing world!

Last but not least, loving and heartfelt thanks to my husband Bruce who is my best friend and has helped me more than words can express.

'Good bye,' said the fox, 'and now here is my secret, a very simple secret.
It is only with the heart, that one can see rightly.
What is essential, is invisible to the eye.'

Antoine de Saint-Exupery, *The Little Prince*

Stress-Free Parenting in 12 Steps

Christiane Kutik

In this concise, practical book Christiane Kutik highlights twelve simple steps for bringing some peace, composure and enjoyment back into everyday family life.

She bases her approach on providing a solid underlying structure to family life, with clear roles, rules, routine and respect. She goes on to show how your family can grow together through incorporating enjoyable rituals, being responsive to your children, giving them the support they need and the space to develop their own abilities.

This is a book written specifically for parents with no time and little energy – short, easy-to-absorb and easy-to-implement steps to quickly improve family life.

www.florisbooks.co.uk

Dyslexia

Learning Disorder or Creative Gift?

Cornelia Jantzen

Dyslexia has long been known as a learning difficulty that primarily affects literacy skills. Increasingly, however, researchers and professionals working with dyslexia suggest that it is less a disorder than a sign of specially gifted people. People with dyslexia often have a highly developed imagination and a unique way of perceiving things. They frequently have above average intelligence and are highly creative, provided they are supported and nurtured by parents and teachers.

In this book Cornelia Jantzen explores the basis of this radical viewpoint. Throughout, she provides many practical examples which explore the different aspects of dyslexia, and can give parents and teachers confidence in dealing with the challenges that it presents.

This is a helpful and encouraging book for anyone looking for new insights into the enigma of dyslexia.

www.florisbooks.co.uk

Why Children Don't Listen

A Guide for Parents and Teachers

Monika Kiel-Hinrichsen

What can you do when a child just won't listen?

How we speak to each other is at the very heart of human relationships. Children are often much better than adults at reading between the lines and deciphering the messages we send through body language and tone of voice.

This is an invaluable handbook for parents and teachers on how to communicate better with children. It covers all aspects of talking to and, importantly, listening to children, including communication with children of different ages and understanding the wider situation in which the conversation is taking place.

The author translates the theory into practical, everyday solutions. There are useful exercises throughout, to help us communicate more successfully.

www.florisbooks.co.uk

Navigating the Terrain of Childhood

A Guidebook for Meaningful Parenting and Heartfelt Discipline

Jack Petrash

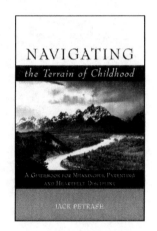

A parent's journey through his or her child's early years is inevitably filled with both precious moments and difficult situations. The unavoidable challenges test us to the limit, and either consume or enlighten us as parents. If we can see these events approaching on the horizon, and prepare for them in advance, the results will be beneficial for both parent and child.

This book is designed to help parents map the terrain that we all travel when raising children, and prepare for the mountains and valleys ahead.

www.florisbooks.co.uk

Addictive Behaviour
in Children and Young Adults

The Struggle for Freedom

Raoul Goldberg

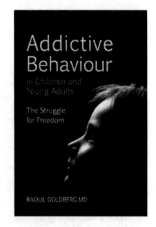

Addiction is one of the most critical problems of our modern world, affecting children as much as adults. We face not only a widespread dependency on illicit substances, but also addictions to food, beverages, cigarettes and alcohol, as well as electronic gadgetry, online social networks, and entertainment media within a culture of violence, along with excessive and unhealthy sexual practices.

This book explores the overall health consequences of addictive behaviour in children and young people, as well as its underlying causes. He examines specific addictions through case histories taken from his clinical practice, and offers a tried and tested method to understand and manage each individual child or young person who succumbs to such dependencies.

This book will be of value to parents, teachers and health professionals who work with children and adolescents.

www.florisbooks.co.uk

Celebrating Festivals with Children

Freya Jaffke

In this thoughtful book, Freya Jaffke describes festival celebrations in relation to child development in the first seven years. She considers in detail the main festivals throughout the year: Easter, Whitsun, St John's, starting school, harvest, Michaelmas, lantern time, birthdays, Halloween, Thanksgiving, Advent, Christmas, Epiphany and carnival.

Drawing on many examples, she shows how we can celebrate festivals with children at home and in kindergarten in a meaningful way. Every festival is prefaced with a deeper contemplation for adults, before considering preparations with children, followed by the actual organisation of the festival – with games, craft activities and decorations, stories, songs, poems and the seasonal nature table.

www.florisbooks.co.uk

Bedtime Storytelling

A Collection for Parents

Beatrys Lockie

What is so special about telling stories? Unlike when reading from a book, you have your arms free to make gestures, use props – or give a tickle. And above all, you have eye contact, so you can observe and respond to your child's reactions. This collection of classic tales includes advice on how to tell stories to children: how to establish a routine and create a mood; how to involve children and personalise your stories.

The stories are suitable for children aged from three to seven years old. Many are old favourites that are regularly told in kindergartens, nurseries and schools – tales about magical creatures and exotic animals as well as stories from everyday life.

Many people say they cannot tell stories, but Beatrys Lockie is a firm believer that everyone can; it just takes a little practice.

www.florisbooks.co.uk